The Master of Achievement.

"There is a powerful driving force inside every human being that, once unleashed, can make any vision, dream, or desire a reality."

— **Anthony Robbins**

scottallan@scottallanpublishing.com

More Bestselling Titles From
Scott Allan

Empower Your Thoughts

Empower Your Deep Focus

Rejection Reset

Rejection Free

Relaunch Your Life

Drive Your Destiny

The Discipline of Masters

Do the Hard Things First

Undefeated

No Punches Pulled

Fail Big

Bite the Bullet

Supercharge Your Best Life

Built for Stealth

Visit author.to/ScottAllanBooks to follow Scott Allan
and stay up to date on future book releases

The

MASTER

OF

ACHIEVEMENT

Conquer Fear and Adversity, Maximize Big Goals,
Supercharge Your Success and Develop a Purpose
Driven Mindset

By Scott Allan

ScottAllan SA
INTERNATIONAL

ISBN eBook: 978-1-989599-04-4

ISBN Paperback: 978-1-989599-30-3

ISBN Hardcover: 978-1-989599-29-7

CONTENTS

JOIN THE COMMUNITY OF 30,000 LIFETIME LEARNERS!

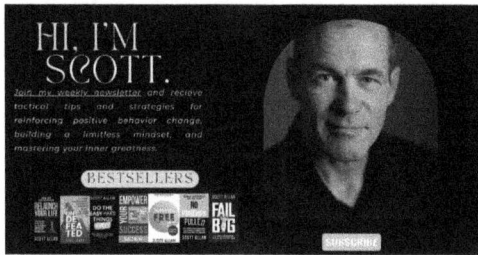

Sign up today for my **free weekly newsletter** and receive instant access to **the** onboarding subscriber pack that includes:

The Fearless Confidence Action Guide: 9 Action Plans for Building Limitless Confidence and Achieving Sustainable Results!

The bestseller poster pack: A poster set of Scott Allan's bestselling books

The Zero Procrastination Blueprint: A Step-by-Step Blueprint to Turn Procrastination into Rapid Action Implementation!

Begin Your Journey and Make This Life Your Own.
Click Here to Subscribe Today **or scan the QR code below.**

Dedication

For Sara and Takumi,
The brightest stars in the universe.

"My mother said to me, "If you become a soldier, you'll be a general; if you become a monk, you'll end up as the Pope." Instead, I became a painter and wound up as Picasso."

Pablo Picasso

The Master of Achievement.

Conquer Fear and Adversity, Maximize **Big Goals**, Supercharge Your **Success** and Develop a Purpose Driven **Mindset**

The Beginning of a Journey

"The only impossible journey is
the one you never begin."

— Tony Robbins

I don't have many good memories of my academic years. In fact, I barely made it through school with enough of a grade to be called passing. Luckily for me, the bar wasn't raised very high. It wasn't that I didn't like school; I just wasn't interested in the courses they offered.

At the end of each academic year, we were tasked with the responsibility of choosing our courses for the next year. I remember asking the teacher if there was another course list to choose from. He just laughed as if I was trying to be funny and went back to marking papers.

I selected six courses, most of which I wasn't interested in. I passed four of them that year. I wasn't a good student. I had a poor attitude and didn't believe academics were going to fix anything. So, I performed at the absolute minimum required to pass. Sometimes I made it and sometimes I didn't. It was like that every year. Choose your courses from this list. What you see is what you get. You don't like the choices? Tough. You'll have to settle for what we have.

This is how we learn early in life to start settling for what people are offering instead of asking for what we want. But when we are forced to choose based on what is available, instead of asking for what we really want, we are being asked to settle for the options. And the options are rarely in our favor.

But I knew in those early days that I wanted more than what was available at the time.

I was always reminded of something John Lennon once said:

"When I was 5 years old, my mom always told me that happiness was the key to life. When I went to school, they asked me what I wanted to be when I grew up. I wrote down "happy." They told me I didn't understand the assignment and I told them they didn't understand life."

I took the available classes because I had no choice. It was either that or go home. When I got to the final year, I was done with school. I had lots of interests, but I couldn't find any of them in academic studies.

When the choices we don't want are forced on us, we take one of two actions: Retaliate, or accept the situation as it is. When you settle for what you can get, you always end up coming up short in life.

To lead the master achievers lifestyle I talk about in this book, we must throw aside all our old habits that pull us back. We must start from the beginning of a new path and take things in a different direction.

Breaking Free of Limitations

A lot of people settle for what's out there instead of building a life and learning to level up as they go. They take the choices available instead of going after what they truly desire. They master jobs they hate and create habits that have no value.

People learn to succeed in things that are not important, which is really the same as failing as you go.

It wasn't until much later that I realized why I had been floundering, drifting, and wasting time all those years.

I had no actionable blueprint for my life. I was drifting through, doing what was expected, and instead of raising the bar, I lowered it in everything I did. The lesson I learned in those days is, what you expect from yourself is what you will end up with in the end.

"There are two types of people who will tell you that you cannot make a difference in this world: those who are afraid to try and those who are afraid you will succeed."

— Ray Goforth

I wasn't engaged in practicing the life lessons that could change everything. I had read lots of books over the years, but they were the wrong books. I had lots of knowledge that I couldn't take action on. A life of settling for mediocrity and believing you should take what you can get isn't the way to build your life. Instead, it stifles it.

That's why we're here. To create a life that has a deeper purpose, with real meaning that makes a difference in the way you think and take action. In my quest to create this life, I made it my mission to discover the core principles that build and develop our emotions, senses, wisdom, and life skills.

On my journey, I came across many works by other authors that helped me break free of limitations and live a life that was superior to what I was being offered.

This book contains ten master strategies to help you live your life in a better way and stop settling for second best. These are strategies that I learned over the years, from rediscovering my mission in life to setting priorities over tasks that waste time.

As you move through this book, you will feel your confidence grow. You will learn to generate a life filled with passion, opportunity, and better relationships. You will learn to fear less while doing more. You will believe that you are here for a grand purpose. You can lead by example through doing instead of just talking about it.

You will discover what you are most passionate about and then develop the action plan to get it done.

The Master of Achievement: What You'll Get on the Inside

The strategies in this book will help you improve the quality of your life, accomplish your goals, and squeeze the most energy out of every day. You will be more energetic, happy, and motivated to do something now.

Can you imagine what your life would be like if you decided to make it your greatest masterpiece? What could you accomplish in one year if you committed yourself to a program of intense instruction that put you at the top of your game?

You have the ability to be and do anything you want. The limits you believe in are yours and yours alone. This means you can destroy them at any time. You have the potential to turn your life into a masterpiece, to develop your skills and turn a dream into a real and very tangible experience.

By modeling the success of other people, by knowing the traits that makes them great and using that as a platform to build on, we can have our own victory. You may not get the same results as everyone else, but your results will be much better because you're doing something rather than nothing.

This book is designed to get you to take massive action. It is about turning confusion into clarity and converting passive thinking into creative ideas that add incredible value to your life. By becoming disciplined in your approach, you will discover what you have always been searching for but could never find. It's not that passion doesn't exist. Rather, you have been looking for it in the wrong places.

If you take a trip and you have a map of the wrong location, you'll be lost before you get off the plane. You need to know where you're going. As we will see in this book, your life is a masterpiece and you are the grand artist.

The Master of Achievement will teach you how to:

- Implement the 16 success traits of highly successful people.

- Create a powerful mission statement.
- Identify the work you are most passionate about.
- Develop a powerful routine that gets things done.
- Utilize my step-by-step process for creating powerful life goals.
- Create the opportunities you want.
- Defeat the ghosts of your past and deal with old resentments keeping you stuck.
- Learn to think like a super-achiever.
- Avoid wasting time by identifying key priority tasks.
- Eliminate distractions that are stealing your energy and focus.
- Remove the internal obstacles still holding you back.
- Find the right mentor and take your success to the next level.
- Overcome deep resentments destroying your relationships.
- Stop wasting time focusing on the little stuff that doesn't matter.
- Learn the "New Challenge Approach" and get past your fear of failure.

How to Read this Book

The Master of Achievement is comprised of ten guiding principles to help you achieve higher levels of success. Each principle stands alone as a valuable lesson. However, all the principles are interconnected as building blocks to success.

Designed to help you get back on track so you aren't wasting time and energy taking action on the wrong things, you will gain a greater sense of purpose and direction. You will experience a greater sense of passion and focus as your thoughts align with what you truly want.

To begin integrating these principles into your life, in the first chapter, you'll learn how to develop a purpose driven mindset. This principle is the foundation for building a life of meaning and value.

Then, in principle two, you will learn to form pro habits with self-discipline and how to apply this in every area of your life. Following this, the principle on goal engineering will walk you through steps for putting together a complete goal portfolio to identify and write down what you're most passionate about achieving.

Principle four focuses on the window of opportunity, which will reveal that life's most valuable lessons are often disguised as failures that lead to success. Principle five discusses adopting a model for success and will show you how choosing a role model adds great value to your life.

Principle six gets into the power of priority planning, which will enable you to identify activities and tasks that demand your attention first. Principle seven focuses in on breaking your obstacles, or "getting over the thirty-foot wall," and shows you the possibilities that manifest when you triumph over life's challenges.

The eighth principle, getting over the past, discusses techniques you can apply to overcome trauma and old thought paradigms that are keeping you stuck.

Principle nine focuses on turning failure into victory, and how you can convert excuses into actionable steps. Learn to talk back to your negative voices and develop the Steve Jobs attitude for success.

The tenth strategy is about building a life beyond fear and doing whatever scares you right now without hesitation. In this chapter you will break the fear keeping you scared and embrace it as your companion on this trip.

Now it is time to empower your life and launch yourself onto the road to success. You are on your way to a greater life than you ever thought possible.

Turn the page and let's start the journey.

The Purpose-Driven Mindset

"The key to realizing a dream is to focus not on success but significance, and then even the small steps and little victories along your path will take on greater meaning."

— Oprah Winfrey

Your life is a journey best fulfilled by determining your purpose, and then pursuing it with rigorous intensity. You are brought into this world with a unique call to action. It is a personal mission that calls for a deeper expression of the life you have been gifted to lead. It is this calling that drives you to master life's valuable principles.

From this moment, consider yourself an artist. This life is to be your greatest creation. You hold the keys to everything you strive to achieve. Everything is yours the moment you accept full responsibility for all of life's successes and failures.

Don't throw away your talents on meaningless activities that waste time. Instead, direct all your mental and physical energy into mastering the one thing that constantly occupies your thoughts.

Make it your mission to integrate this passion into everything you do. What you focus on is what you become. What you take action on defines your real purpose. The thoughts and dreams that keep you awake at night are directing you to take action towards a higher purpose. As Robert Schuller said, "You are what you think about all day long." So, what do you think about all the time that won't rest? Whatever it is, pay attention to it. Listen to the guidance it is pushing towards you.

Focus on performing the right actions and you'll do the right thing. Allow nothing to pull you off course, and when it does, you will have the focus and clarity to correct your course. You are, at all times, the master of fate in control of your own life vessel.

The Master of Talents

Our living purpose is revealed to us in many ways. It could be a deep interest in a particular field of study, a burning passion for music, the arts or theater. You might have the burning desire to pursue a career in medicine, education or politics.

Your passion could lie in helping people discover ways to improve the quality of their lives, participating in global events that shape the future for new generations, or joining an organization dedicated to a valuable cause. You may have a desire to master languages, play a particular musical instrument, or play a sport.

Whatever it is that is calling to you now, I encourage you to move towards it. Embrace this passion and pursue it with everything you've got. You must learn to live creatively by designing a dream for your life that fully expresses who you are and why you are here.

As children, passions are prevalent in the interests we pick up, the skills developed at an early age, or the special talents that make us shine brighter than the rest as we discover our unique calling. Some children struggle to live normal childhoods and to be like other children as their calling to fulfill a special mission feels like a heavy burden. They begin planning their future from a young age, practicing their craft with relentless diligence and concentration until mastered.

You can see these people as gifted geniuses and the young prodigies that excel in their selected areas of interest. They become masters of the skills that drive them to pursue life's purpose without fear or hesitation.

It is your purpose in this life that has brought you here. It is your life's quest to discover and develop this. You have a message to deliver, and it is your calling to share this message with the world. To take the path of least resistance—the path of ignorance and unconsciousness—is to ignore your mission.

Don't live below your potential. Don't settle for what is "good enough." Instead, push yourself to rise above self-created limitations. Question the voices of doubt and challenge yourself to follow your path.

Expanding Infinite Choices

You are one of a kind. There is nobody else like you in this world. If you are a writer, you write in your own way. If you are a pianist, you play the way that best suits your style. If you are a painter, your unique abilities will shine through in everything you create. You can choose to perform in any style or fashion you desire.

"Stop chasing the money and start chasing the passion."

— Tony Hsieh

Let's take the example of two talented musicians. Although they might play the same type of music, both musicians are different. They have their own style and method of self-expression as it is portrayed through their music. This is the same with any role that is played in life. It is not the role you play, but how you play it. It is not the instrument that matters, but the talent that masters it.

Be the master of your own unique talents and work to make your music heard. You are unique, and everything you do is going to have your signature applied to it. Even if someone attempts to copy what you have done, they will never be able to produce the same results.

There are always infinite choices in relation to the pathways available to you. Every new road leads to a new experience, and the pathways you choose to take determine the experiences you will have. It's critical not to regret the events of the past or dwell on things that cannot be undone.

Focus on the now and make today count. By staying in the present, you are in a stronger position to connect with your purpose.

Make a firm decision about what you want to accomplish, the values you are choosing to live by, and the principles to guide you to where you need to be. Finally, focus all your attention on achieving whatever would have the greatest impact on what matters most to you.

Sixteen Strategies for Super-Charging Your Success

"The path to our destination is not always a straight one. We go down the wrong road, we get lost, we turn back. Maybe it doesn't matter which road we embark on. Maybe what matters is that we embark."

— Barbara Hall

The greatest challenge we face these days is the quest for a deeper meaning. Many people have become lost in the diversification of complexities. In an age of massive information output, we exist in a world that is growing increasingly more complex. As a result, we are finding it harder to establish and maintain cultural values that are congruent with the true nature of our identity.

If you take the time to study the lives of great men and women throughout the centuries, you will find a common thread. They are bound by a set of common principles that molds their success into legacy and legend.

High-level super-achievers—those who have mastered greatness by committing to living their purpose—focus their thoughts, total attention, and enthusiasm into mastering a skill. They are craftsmen, and their accomplishments remain an inspiration.

They have learned the secret formula: To develop a purpose-driven mindset by determining what they want and then exercising all efforts toward the successful completion of that objective.

Here are sixteen key strategies that super-achievers with a purpose-driven mindset put into practice in order to achieve success and gain greater self-mastery in every area of their lives.

1. Total Commitment to a Worthy Objective

Purpose-driven individuals are committed to fulfilling an objective. Commitment is the first step toward making consistent progress and turning an idea into an actionable goal that gets massive results.

Fulfilling your life's mission isn't an event that happens by accident. It requires a deeper commitment to taking action on a daily basis. It is knowing what you want. It is also knowing WHY you want it and following through with the right actions to get it done.

What goals are you committed to that would create serious change in your life today? If you commit to an objective every morning and focus on what matters most, what is the new reality that you would be able to create?

What habits and daily actions are you ready to commit to over the long-term? Are you ready to start your journey from today?

Learn more about living a purpose-driven life by reading The Road Less Traveled: A New Psychology of Love, Traditional Values and Spiritual Growth by M. Scott Peck.

2. Clearly Defined Goals and Objectives

Purpose-driven people have clearly defined goals. With your goals in clear sight and an actionable plan for how you'll get there, you can turn anything into a positive result.

Goals are like beacons in the ocean that guide ships toward safety. With your goals and objectives clearly planned, you'll get where you need to be. The rest will drift in the tide.

What goals are you most passionate about? How can you inject this passion into achieving your life's vision? Is there a master goal you have longed to achieve but put it on the back burner to "simmer" while life passes by?

We will take a look at goal setting more in chapter four, and you will be able to set up your own goal portfolio in a matter of hours.

For more information on setting goals, I recommend you read Brian Tracy's book Maximum Achievement: Strategies and Skills That Will Unlock Your Hidden Powers to Succeed.

3. Diligent Work Ethic

Purpose-driven people work hard until the task is complete, without considering the number of hours they will need to spend on it. While most people are clock watchers, world-class achievers often don't think of clocking in or out. They work until they have completed their objectives. They are committed 100 percent to working long hours and putting in the necessary effort to succeed.

Bill Gates, the founder of Microsoft, once said, "In my twenties I never took a day off." Bill Gates had clearly defined goals and a mission.

What is your mission?
What are you working toward?
Do you want to work for a paycheck, or would you rather work toward fulfilling your dreams?

Decide right now what you love to do more than anything else, and then organize all your actions around this.

For more information on working diligently and increasing productivity, I recommend David Allen's bestselling book Getting Things Done.

4. Organized Actions Supported by a Long-Term Plan

Purpose-driven people are committed to working diligently toward their dreams with actionable intent. They organize all activities, thoughts, and actions toward defining this singleness of purpose. They have an organized plan.

The individual with a purpose-driven mind has a list of actionable items that must be completed according to the objectives they are working toward.

What actions could you take every day that would have a significant impact on your life one month from now? What actions could you start doing tomorrow that would change everything if you continued on this course for 90 days?

Instead of following someone else's plan for your life, what is the plan you would create in alignment with your passions?

For a detailed script on long-term planning, I recommend Michael Hyatt's Living Forward: A Proven Plan to Stop Drifting and Get the Life You Want.

5. Persistence in the Face of Defeat

Purpose-driven people do not give up. They perceive failure as a necessary pathway to a successful outcome. Failing is the road to success.

Persistence plays a vital role in succeeding at anything you have a desire to accomplish. For successful people, facing failure and overcoming fears to break through obstacles is the only way to win.

What obstacles do you face? Are these barriers going to stop you from living your life as it could be?

Take a look at an obstacle in your life that is slowing your progress and map out a list of solutions you can apply today to begin working through it.

Take the best solution and put it into action. If it doesn't work, try another solution. Keep working on this until you overcome this surmountable barrier. More often than not, most obstacles that defeat you are bigger in your mind than they really appear.

For a deeper look at overcoming obstacles, I recommend The Obstacle is the Way by Ryan Holiday

6. Consistent and Disciplined Habits

Successful people are disciplined. They train themselves to develop the right habits needed to reach the outcomes they want. Like the carpenter who selects the proper tools for the job, you have to select the proper habits that meet your desired outcome.

If you want to open a business, you should learn about the tactics and strategies successful business leaders implement. Do you want to get into better shape? Make it a habit of waking up early and doing twenty minutes of exercise. Do you want to save money? Create the habit of spending less.

What are some negative habits you have that rob you of energy, time, and motivation? What is the one habit you could implement from today that would deliver life-changing results if you practiced it for thirty days?

Make a list of the habits you want to change. Then, make a list of the new habits you will integrate from this week and work toward making them a part of your life. By creating just one new habit, you could change the course of your life.

For more information on developing habits, I recommend you read Charles Duhigg's The Power of Habit: Why We Do What We Do in Life and Business.

7. Effective Time Management

Purpose-driven people possess a positive mental attitude, casting aside all negative doubts, self-limitations, and dependence on outside influence for the level of success they can accomplish. Creating a positive mental attitude is essential. Everything you experience will flow from this mental state.

By managing your actions and being clear about objectives and goals, you will funnel every effort into using your time to be more productive.

Do you spend your time effectively, or do you waste it when you know there is something more important you should be doing?

Establish the actions you want to take that contribute toward building life skills and feed your greatest passion. By organizing your actions around a worthy cause, your time management issues will resolve themselves.

For more information on building a system of efficient time management, I recommend Stephen Covey's The 7 Habits of Highly Effective People.

8. Positive Mental Attitude

Purpose-driven people possess a superior positive mental attitude, casting aside all negative doubts, self-limitations, and dependence on outside influence for the level of success they can accomplish. Creating a positive mental attitude (PMA) is essential. Everything you experience will flow from this positive mental state.

Negative thinking destroys creativity, creates unnecessary worry, and limits the course of success. Master achievers do not follow this path. They are positive thinkers and can find the good in even the worst possible situation. Instead of drowning in negative emotions and self-doubt that inhibit so many from tapping into their full potential, those who succeed work hard to avoid negativity.

Make a conscious effort to monitor your thoughts and attitude toward people, places, and things. If you discover a negative frame of mind is blocking your ability to move forward, you now have a place from which to start building your success platform.

Are you a positive person, or do you have a tendency to think the worst about situations, people, and yourself in general? Are you in control of your thoughts, or are they controlling you? Is worry creating more stress and fear in your life?

For more information on adopting a positive mental state, I recommend you read Napoleon Hill's Keys to Success: The 17 Principles of Personal Achievement.

9. Opportunity Builders

Purpose-driven people create their own opportunities, which lead to successful outcomes. They create the desired circumstances for fulfilling their sense of purpose and achieving their dreams and objectives.

Master achievers are opportunity seekers. They are open-minded and willing to explore new opportunities that expand on wealth, knowledge, and self-development.

For example, successful entrepreneurs create the products they want to use. Instead of waiting for it to happen, they make it happen. The best opportunity of your life could be the one that you forge yourself. Why wait for someone to bring it to you?

People who wait for opportunity end up employed by others. But when you set up the circumstances to deliver what you need, you can employ others to make it happen.

What new opportunities could you create for yourself that would open doors to wealth, health, and success? Is there an opportunity you want, but haven't yet figured out how to attract? What actions could you take that would invite this opportunity into your life? Who could you connect with that would help open these opportunities?

For a deeper read on building more opportunity in your business and your life, I recommend you read Good to Great by Jim Collins.

10. Future Visionaries

Purpose-driven master achievers are visionaries. They direct all thoughts and actions toward making this vision a concrete reality. They see the big picture and share this vision with everyone involved. Their minds are constantly at work creating what the future will be once they have completed their work.

All thoughts, actions, and behaviors are directed toward making this vision a reality.

Do you have a vision for your life? Where do you imagine you will be emotionally, spiritually, and financially in ten years? How about twenty years?

Take some time for quiet contemplation. An hour spent thinking about and imagining the life you desire is equivalent to eight hours of hard work.

For more information on learning to visualize, I recommend Creative Visualization by Shakti Gawain.

11. Build Effective Support Teams

Successful people surround themselves with an alliance of winners to share ideas and discuss the solution to problems. Together they work to overcome adversity.

They are interested in forging powerful partnerships with people who have similar goals and ambitions. Purpose-driven successors forge serious and lasting relationships by bonding with those who are interested in making a difference.

Are you surrounded by a team of winners who support what you do? Or do you work in an environment that robs you of creativity, fills you with negativity, and contributes more to your lack of success than anything else?

If the people you engage with are holding you back, it is time to consider forging new relationships. If you do, this will contribute to building your positive mental state and create different levels of opportunity.

To build greater success in your work and your life, I recommend you read Deep Work: Rules for Focused Success in a Distracted World by Cal Newport.

12. Superior Belief System

Successful people have unshakeable faith in what they can achieve. They believe in their mission, ideas, and purpose. Regardless of obstacles or challenges, they are confident that anything can be overcome if they believe it can be. They have the foundational belief that they will succeed and they will do anything to manifest the outcome they desire.

Most people set limits on themselves because of limiting beliefs. They create limited income, limit their abilities, and limit their learning skills.

But successful people are limitless in their pursuits. They continue to grow, expand, develop, and reach out to breach the horizons untouched by the masses.

What do you believe in? Do you believe that success is a matter of luck or chance? Or do you believe anything can happen if you trust the possibilities? Your beliefs, like habits, forge a powerful alliance with destiny.

For more information on creating beliefs, I recommend Unlimited Power by Anthony Robbins.

13. Dedicated to Continuous Self-Improvement

Purpose-driven people are constant learners. They learn and continuously adapt from their mistakes. They quickly pick up new skills to stay connected with the changing times. They are always improving their mental attitudes and sharpening leadership, relationship, and management skills to foster further growth.

A constant and never-ending commitment to self-development is the foundation of successful people.

How can you make improvements to your life starting today? Could you acquire a new skill? Listen to a weekly podcast from a top-notch motivational speaker? Read new material on character development?

There are literally hundreds of ways you can make small improvements to your life that would have a major impact if you are committed.

Set a goal to focus on one area of your life you can develop for both your mindset and your business. Commit to developing this principle or value by focusing on the one thing that can make a difference in your life tomorrow.

For more on continuous self-improvement, I recommend you read The Success Principles by Jack Canfield.

14. Focused Concentration on Priority Tasks

Purpose-driven individuals are focused on the tasks at hand. They do not waver or become consumed by daily trivial activities. They don't allow themselves to be pulled down by a negative attitude, griping, harsh criticisms, or undirected thinking that leads to the loss of self-control. They are focused on important matters that make a difference.

Do you find yourself lost in complaints about small things that don't matter? If so, how can you direct your thoughts and emotions toward more important issues?

What are the daily gripes you are consumed by? How can you stop engaging in trivial matters that don't contribute to your overall self-improvement?

By recognizing the one thing we shouldn't be focusing on, we free up more space and energy to stay fixed on the tasks that really matter.

To read more about creating fewer distractions, I recommend The One Thing by Gary Keller.

15. Do the Things Most People Avoid

Albert Gray said, "Successful people are successful because they form the habits of doing those things that failures don't like to do." This is the most defining characteristic that separates people who do what they love to do from those who do what they are made to do by others.

People live life as an expression of the choices they have made when they do what others are afraid to. Your actions define you. Do what needs to be done, for as long as it takes, and you will have very little competition.

Is there an action you have been avoiding because you're afraid of failing? Are you procrastinating?

Remember, you will have a much better chance to live life your way when you do the work most people turn away from.

Make a short list of five actions you can take this week that will have a major impact on your performance. Then, from that list, choose only one task and focus on it for ninety days. Make this action key to pushing your momentum to its peak.

For more on achieving greater success, read The Common Denominator of Success by Albert Gray.

16. Create the Circumstances You Want

Purpose-driven people can adapt to sudden changes in the economy, environment, or circumstances. They are not overcome by changes beyond their control. Instead, they adapt to shifting situations.

Many people just go with the flow whereas purpose-driven people create the flow they desire. They create the changes they want to see happen instead of just letting it happen to them. They adapt and change course when needed. It is an inevitable part of the process.

Do you like change, or are you afraid of it? How do you adapt to sudden changes in the workplace or at home? Always keep this one truth in mind: Change is inevitable.

Everything you are experiencing today will be completely different ten years from now. It may be completely different tomorrow. But you don't have to wait for things to change. You can take control today and create the changes you want instead of waiting for them to happen.

For more on learning to implement change, I recommend Switch by Chip Heath and Dan Heath.

Execute the Strategies

You now have sixteen strategies you can start working on right now. I would suggest you focus on just one at a time. Once you have mastered each one, go back to the beginning and start again.

People who live their dreams have defined their purpose and are living out their greatest passions. For them, success comes through living the life they were meant to live by making the necessary choices that are in alignment with the fulfillment of goals, principles, and values. They spend their days creating, building and living their dreams, not just dreaming of an illusory life that could be.

You must pursue this path if you are to develop your connected purpose.

Mission Statement: Building a Deeper Meaning into Your Life

"Definiteness of purpose is the starting point of all achievement."

— W. Clement Stone

Once you are clear about what brings you the greatest joy and fulfillment, your purpose will be defined through the everyday actions organized around your life's purpose and mission. The surest way to bring your life's path into alignment with your purpose is by creating a personal mission statement—a concise statement that defines your focus.

At the top of a piece of paper, write out the following: The Purpose of My Life.

Next, write down what you believe the purpose of your life is, in as many words as it takes. Ask yourself specific questions to get things started. Below is a list of twenty questions for you to think about that can generate powerful ideas leading to the answers you seek.

Now, take the time to write out your answers. There is a lot of work involved here, so you should give yourself two to three days to finish this.

Once complete, think carefully about what you have written down, and then create a clear, concise statement that defines the nature of your life's purpose and mission.

- What are my strongest areas of interest? If I had to commit to mastering just one area of my life, what would it be?
- What coincidences have occurred in my life that might be trying to tell me something?
- How would I spend the rest of my days if I could do absolutely anything I wanted? If making money wasn't important, what is the one thing I would do for free if I could?

- What is a particular field of interest that I feel drawn to? Do I think often about this interest, even when I'm engaged in other work?

- As a child, what were the creative activities I enjoyed most? Do I still feel drawn to these things?

- What kind of person would I like to emulate in regard to talent, inspiration, or social impact? Is it an artist, writer, global leader, or business entrepreneur? What is it about this person that I admire most?

- How would I define the nature of my personality? Am I intuitive, creative, humorous, or a serious thinker?

- What are three things I like about my personality? What are three things I don't like and would like to change?

- What is the one thing in my life that, if I changed it, would have a significant impact on the quality of my life?

- What is the one thing I would like to contribute to the world? How would this contribution add value to the lives of others?

- Is there a person whom I could help to achieve success, or to somehow better themselves? If so, who is it, and what could I do for that person?

- If I were to accomplish my life's pursuit, how would it benefit the world, my community, and my friends and family?

- What are the values I hold most sacred? What new values would I have to adopt in order to live in alignment with my life's purpose?

- How do I feel about myself in terms of self-worth, confidence, and quality of character?

- Following up on the previous question, how can I make improvements to my self-worth, confidence, and the quality of my character?

- Do I experience long periods of emptiness, numbness, or absolute hopelessness? If so, how often does this occur? What do I think are the causes for these dark emotions? Is it a lack of purpose, a loss of faith, or the feeling that my life has no meaning?

- What are five things I am most grateful for? How would I feel if these things were taken from me? What would I be willing to do to keep these gifts of gratitude in my life?

- What are three things I regret not doing in my life? What is the one thing I would regret not accomplishing if I don't take action today?
- Am I happy where I am in my life today? Is there anything I can change so that I can enjoy a better quality of life?

Putting the Plan Together

The next step is to clearly define, in writing, your living purpose statement. This expresses what you are going to do with your life on a larger scale.

Read through each of the following sections and answer the questions as best you can.

Define the kind of person you want to become.

You are defined by the difference you make in the lives of the people around you. You further define yourself through self-expression and your attitude toward people and events. Now, take a moment to answer the following questions in your notebook. When you have finished, read over and reflect on what you have written.

- What ideas or thoughts do you have about yourself?
- What do others think of you? Is their assessment of you accurate? How do you see yourself?
- What would someone say about you if they were speaking about you to other people?
- In what ways do you contribute to the happiness and well-being of others?
- What kind of person do you see yourself evolving into over the next decade?
- How would you define yourself in terms of character traits, personal values, beliefs, and ambitions?
- What are the most important things in your life today?
- Who is it that contributes to your joy and well-being?
- If you could change just one thing about yourself, what would it be?

- If you could change just one thing in this world, what would it be?

Define the Work You Want to Do.

Meaningful work contributes to the joy and happiness of others, while also contributing to the world in ways that greatly influence growth and change. There is an ocean of unlimited opportunities available to you.

Many paths are presented to each of us every day. However, they are often unseen because we are so wrapped up in performing the tasks that others have set out for us. Your inherent talent that has yet to be discovered is one of the key elements that could potentially unlock your success.

Discover the work that drives you, fills you with enthusiasm, and infuses passion into every action you take.

- What kind of work do you enjoy doing? Is it something creative, mechanical, or educational?
- Is there any kind of work that makes you completely forget about the clock? In other words, have you ever become so absorbed in some kind of work that you completely lost track of time?
- Can you see yourself becoming successful in this line of work? If not, why?
- What area of expertise would put you on a direct course with your ultimate goals and sense of purpose?
- Do you have any talents that could develop into a joyful and fulfilling career if you applied yourself to exercising this talent in a way that generated income?
- What could you do today to start developing these talents?

Define Your Master Talent.

Like an abundant treasure just waiting to be discovered, everybody has at least one special talent they could master and contribute to the world. The first sight of a piano attracts a would-be musician;

an artist, upon seeing paint and color for the first time, instantly perceives an image that must be canvassed; and a builder wants to create a beautiful structure.

If you want to attain a level of happiness and satisfaction beyond your wildest dreams, do whatever prompts your interest. Follow your passion and that is where you will discover your greatest joy.

- What talent or skill do you feel a strong attraction to? Is it in the field of writing, business, education, or art?
- Is there something that beckons you to take action, something that urges you to pick up a hobby or study something new? Do you have a keen interest in something profound, but you don't yet know or understand why?
- Is there something you have always had a high aptitude for?
- Are you drawn toward certain activities you feel compelled to pursue?
- What activities or work do you engage in that make you completely lose all track of time?
- Is there something that you were always better at than everybody else? If so, what is it?

Define Your Greatest Passion.

Passion is key! Do what keeps you energized, enthusiastic, and motivated. Passion is the main element in constructing a life with great purpose.

Passion involves doing something with a strong sense of self-love. Your great purpose should be linked to your passions. Without passion, there can be no purpose.

The purpose of your life and the reasons for your existence breathe energy into everything you do. Do the things you love and do them as often as you can.

Write it! The Great Purpose Statement

The final stage has come for you to put your great purpose into words. Once you have determined your purpose by defining your greatest passions, intuitions, and natural talents, you will begin attracting all the valuable resources, people, and rich ideas that you need for fulfilling your dreams.

A great purpose, once defined, begins to work right away in fulfilling your needs and providing you with the support required to make it happen. You will experience great changes and an absolute sense of belonging—a connection to something more profound than anything you have ever felt before.

Referring to the questions you answered above about your great purpose, put everything together into a working purpose statement.

Take a few moments of quiet time to reflect on the importance of your purpose. Seek answers to questions deep within yourself. Look for the inner truth that has yet to reveal itself. Meditate or take a long walk and think clearly with a peaceful mind about the purpose of everything you are destined to do and be.

When you are ready, write down your great purpose in your notebook. Write only as much as is necessary. Then, read over it again and delete what you don't need. Your goal is to create a concise, snappy statement that is easy to remember. It should also be inspiring and lift you up every time you read it.

Once your great purpose statement is finalized, read it at least twice every day. Doing so will feed your conscious and subconscious mind with powerful words, thoughts, and visions that build the foundations of your life purpose.

Everyone has creative gifts and deep passions lying dormant within just waiting to be discovered. Once discovered, these special gifts will be shared with the world in the form of art, music, business, literature, speeches and more.

Rise to the Challenge: Your Call to Action!

Now, how can you develop a purpose-driven mindset to unveil what remains to be discovered within yourself? How can you, from this moment on, start building your dreams and living the life you were meant to live? How can you gain mastery over your thoughts and actions to steer your life in the direction it is intended to take?

Now is the time to get serious about the things you're passionate about. Search with a clear mind to reignite the dreams that you have long since buried and forgotten. Bring back to life the part of you that has been abandoned.

Plan for attaining the goals you once considered impossible and get to work immediately to make them real. Adopting just one of the strategies from the list already presented will make a dramatic difference in the quality of your success.

By developing a purpose-driven mindset, you will steer a course of action that generates the positive energy necessary for beginning the greatest journey of your life. Work to discover what you have a natural talent for and concentrate to master your greatest passion.

Know precisely what you want and discard what no longer holds any value for you. Establish your desired outcome with absolute clarity and then commit all of your available resources to pursuing the life you yearn to live. Put your purpose-driven mindset into full throttle and turn your passions into your greatest quest.

Accept nothing but the best for yourself and raise personal expectations to exceed all false limitations and beliefs. Hold yourself accountable. Make a promise to yourself to live each day with a greater purpose in all your thoughts, intentions and actions.

Self-Discipline and Building Better Habits

"In reading the lives of great men, I found that the first victory they won was over themselves…self-discipline with all of them came first."

— Harry S. Truman

When you build self-discipline, you are training the mind, body, and spirit. This builds a solid foundation for maximum performance, setting the stage for greater success.

Apply self-discipline to master key areas of your business or develop stronger family relationships. With discipline, you can boost earning power, design a new product, or lift your career to a new level.

With the application of the correct tools, techniques, and skills, everything you desire is attracted to you. The highest vision you hold for yourself becomes your reality when you apply a set of specific and concrete actions geared toward living life in a disciplined manner.

Commitment by Choice

To be disciplined in your daily activities is to be trained in the art of doing what matters most first, in order to accomplish your primary goals and objectives.

Those who have learned to direct mental power in a disciplined way will surpass their expectations and overcome all self-imposed limitations. These people are in tune with the diligence needed to overcome all obstacles and persevere.

By forming positive habits, you set the course to find fulfillment. This means being in control, taking charge, and making choices that lead to significant changes in thoughts, actions, and behavior.

By making the decision, you can do what most people refuse to do, and that gives you the necessary edge. When you are committed to going that extra mile, you no longer crave the easy way. You accept the difficulties that lie ahead, you are open to the truth that nothing comes for free, and that anything worth attaining is going to require sacrifice and a conscious effort to maintain this diligence.

When we accept that life is hard and not always fair, we are open to the idea that everything is driven by the power of choice. You can choose to live as you always have, or you can choose to adopt a new set of principles and habits that foster change.

Instead of performing work just for the sake of keeping busy, your actions will be driven by your purpose. Your passion becomes an unbreakable obsession.

We must constantly focus on ridding ourselves of any negativity that makes us ill. Old thoughts must be replaced. Destructive habits must be cast aside and new habits created. The old ways that no longer serve the vision you hold for yourself must be replaced by a new set of strategies. If you do these things with consistency, commitment to creating an empowering life will become the cornerstone of purposeful living.

Integrating Habits into Daily Living

The core of any discipline begins with controlled action. Integrating habits with purpose leads to successful results. When you are in control of your best habits, you can effectively master anything you set out to learn. If you're looking to redefine the way you're spending your life, take a look at the habits occupying your time.

Ask yourself:
- How can I do this better, more efficiently, or more creatively?
- What habits do I need to create to get what I want?
- Do I have any habits that are lessening my chances for a better future?

The habits you form today will define who you are. Match your choices with habits that lead toward living your ideal lifestyle.

For example, if you want to have more money, but compulsive shopping is a problem, you need to create a system in which you are saving money regularly.

Adjust your behavior and you'll see a different result. Perform the right kind of behavior in alignment with your goals and you'll find the formula for success.

"If you will discipline yourself to make your mind self-sufficient you will thereby be least vulnerable to injury from the outside."

— Critias of Athens

Negative habits like excessive television watching become automatic reactions when you have time alone. The result is lost opportunity, money, and freedom as you become a slave to your weaker impulses.

If you spend a lot of time watching TV, that means less time exercising, reading, meditating, writing, or working on your dreams. You are exchanging future fulfillment for temporary pleasure.

There is nothing wrong with enjoying some television, but when it takes the place of fulfilling our dreams, we are trading our futures for the sake of entertainment.

The habits you choose to live by are made through smart choices. Be sure to choose what is best for your growth and self-development.

Letting Go of the Material World

Going without the things we want to own is considered a form of personal deprivation in today's world. Many people eat what they want, buy what they want, and possess whatever they want through any means necessary.

Advertising and marketing campaigns have made it quite clear that the wait is over. Thanks to credit cards, there's no need to hold out for a well-paying job before owning everything we desire. As long as you have the basic means to cover the minimum monthly fee (not the principle), you can own whatever you want and do whatever your heart desires.

With the right connections, the world and everything in it is ours for the taking. Sadly, many people have bought into this alternate reality and the "buy now, pay later" mindset.

We have adopted the attitude that to live without is to be without. This, combined with poor spending habits, has reinforced the path of least resistance. The result is a complete loss of control with very little discipline for managing our lifestyle or financial future.

Learning to live without is simply learning to say no to impulsive, irresponsible actions so that you can say yes to something positive. Learning to live without is learning to live with more—more choices, more freedom, more money, and more time.

Overindulgence is one of the biggest downfalls of hard-working people. When you focus on overcoming compulsive habits, you will discover a new freedom and a better way of life.

When you make a conscious choice to follow your path, your old life will fall away. You are free to reinvent yourself in any way you like.

When we condition ourselves to live without, we gain more. Decide today that you are going to fill up your life with the riches of harmony and joy. Cast aside addiction to material objects. Become someone who gives more to others. Your life will expand to include better choices and opportunity, richer relationships based on trust, and friendships that last a lifetime.

Instead of trying to acquire more stuff, seek to attract more positive influences into your life. Build higher quality relationships and you will become more fulfilled in ways you never imagined. The fulfillment you seek already exists within, so there is no need to go looking for it.

Breaking Resistance

Putting off vital tasks that are uncomfortable turns into a poor habit that supports the quick fix addiction. The things we avoid are still there the next day.

There is a strong attraction to take the path of least resistance. Instead of doing what we don't want to do and getting it over with, we procrastinate.

Here are two suggestions to get you moving. Remember that when you put something on the back burner, it eventually goes up in flames.

1. Do the one thing you resist, first

Make a list of tasks you've been avoiding. Ask yourself why. Is it because there is paperwork involved, or a phone call you'll have to make that you've been dreading? People resist doing things for what they feel are good reasons. They know this reason, even if they haven't admitted it to themselves.

Do not allow yourself to make self-defeating excuses. Once you start down this road, the habits you will develop over the years will determine your success or failure. If you develop good habits based on achieving specific goals, you will reach that successful plateau in your life. But if you are feeding into bad habits that rob you of your health, finances, or steal your time away, the results you get will drag you down and failure will be your experience.

Always strive to build the habits that make a positive difference in your life and the lives of other people.

By committing to doing one thing every day that you don't feel like doing, and completing it, you build the strands of a new habit. If you do this repeatedly for thirty days, your resistance will turn to persistence and you will no longer be making excuses as to why you should be doing something.

Instead, you will be making good reasons why it needs to be done right away. And the best part is, once the task is finished, you will have taken control of a big part of your life that was out of control. There is nothing that feels better than knowing you have the power to make choices that govern your own life. Imagine how you would feel after completing the task.

You may discover that the path of least resistance carries no merit. You are avoiding doing things that in fact build your confidence and make you feel better about yourself. Instead of putting things off, form the habit of doing the toughest item on your list first.

Do anything that contributes to progress, whether it means filling out a necessary form or making an outline for a business meeting on Monday. Put the ball in forward motion and do anything that gets you working toward completing your task.

Imagine the project completed. See yourself succeeding at every turn. Imagine what it would be like knowing you have tackled the task, finished it, and now you can take a break and do anything you desire—because you took care of business first.

Developing this habit is the essence of integrating discipline into your daily action plan.

2. Challenge your comfort zone

Most of us live within the confines of a small box. It is in this space that we feel at home, comfortable, unchallenged, and at ease. If you have ever stepped outside this zone, you likely experienced fear, anxiety, or insecurity.

People who stay within limited boundaries rarely make any significant progress. The comfort zone suppresses your potential. Skills remain undeveloped, talents wither and fade, and the mind and body grows lethargic with boredom.

Decide right now to do something every day that challenges you to step out of your safety zone. Try something new. Do something you've always wanted to try. Join a gym or take a course you've been putting off. Challenge your greatest fear and push hard when you come up against resistance. If you do it once, you will eventually create a new habit for taking on any challenge that comes your way.

Right now, make a list of things you have been resisting. Once you have your list, decide on something you are going to do right away. You will feel out of place and your instinct may be to run and retreat but don't do that until you've given it your everything.

Get into the habit of doing things you've always wanted to do, but always feared attempting. The outcome of this habit may lead to life changing events.

Five Habits to Building Better Discipline

"Discipline is the bridge between goals and accomplishment."

— Jim Rohn

1. Develop a Plan

In order to train yourself to get the important tasks done first, you have to have a plan for achieving these things. This can be the development of a project you are working on, or the action steps required to complete a long-term goal. Right now, take out a pen, highlighters, and paper. In the middle of the page, write down the goal or dream you are passionate about pursuing. Now highlight your goal.

Next, brainstorm all the steps you can think of that are necessary to achieving this goal. Don't worry about the order. You can fill in the details later. Flush out all the ideas and actions that come to mind as you think about this work. Now, on a separate page, organize your thoughts further by writing out the steps needed to carry out these tasks.

2. Commit to Working Toward Your Plan

A calendar or schedule book would be convenient at this stage. I use a wall calendar to plan my week and my tasks. This is a great form of self-discipline: Getting organized!

Now that you have a list of actions, ordered by priority, you can start penciling in the steps on a calendar. The calendar will serve as a reminder of the actions you are focusing on.

Once you know what to do, it is a matter of committing to it. Know what you have to do, commit yourself to the plan, and then....

3. Follow Through with Consistent Action

Get busy. Once you commit to your plan, stick with it. The longer you work the action steps and move closer to achieving your goals, the more you will have defeated the path of least resistance. It isn't enough just to do something every now and then and expect to improve. It has to be consistent. Work until it's finished.

There is a world of difference between somebody who sits down to practice the piano whenever they feel like it, as opposed to doing it with a set schedule that puts them in the practice seat almost daily.

Consistency is the key to molding a habit. The actions you fix your focus on over a long period of time determine the results you accomplish. By devoting 10 to 20 minutes a day toward mastering a specific skill set, you can set this habit on autopilot after 60 days.

Implement the Seinfeld strategy and use a wall calendar to mark an "action taken" for each day. If you exercise that day, put a check on the calendar for that day. But miss a day and nothing gets checked. Don't break the chain method which builds consistency.

4. Manage Your Minutes

Perhaps the greatest test of a person's disciplinary power is their ability to effectively manage time. Your time is the most limited and precious resource you have. It is more important than money, because even though you can afford to waste your hard-earned cash, time is the one resource you cannot afford to lose. Every day counts.

Keeping a rigorous schedule helps manage your time. When you commit time to a project or task, you are investing in that activity.

The discipline to apply your time and organize it toward actions that make a difference in building the quality of your life is what separates achievers from the drifters.

People who are disorganized and have failed to acknowledge the actions they need to commit to on a daily basis suffer a great loss.

They drift from one idea to the next, and one interest to another, without really committing to anything.

In order to manage your time effectively, you must know with accurate precision the actions that need to be taken. Then set aside the time to do the work.

For the rest of the week, take a project or task you have been putting off, or something you've been meaning to start but haven't gotten around to yet. Block off a chunk of time and commit to working during that block of time. Don't stop concentrating your efforts until the time is up.

Do this for several days and you will have formed the fine strands of a good habit. Do it repetitively for several weeks and those strands will form into unbreakable cables. You will find that your most precious resource is being used to its maximum efficiency.

5. Take Daily Inventory

Before going to sleep, take a few minutes to review your day. Look at the problems, challenges, and situations you faced and make mental notes of the methods you used to deal with these challenges. How could you have reacted differently? Was the problem resolved, or is it still unfinished?

Take a look at your interactions with people and come up with ideas you can use to improve your communication with them. Make this step a daily habit! This is one of the most important exercises you will do because it is a great way to clean your slate. It will provide you with some perspective as to how you deal with situations and where your weaknesses are in relation to your strengths.

Action Plan

1. In what areas of your life do you require the greatest self-discipline? Is it your job, family, physical exercise, eating habits, or finances?

2. How can you apply the principle of discipline to make changes in any or all of these areas?

3. Who is responsible for teaching you about self-discipline? What are the habits you have acquired that you would like to change? How are you going to change these habits?

4. What are some core characteristics that separate successful people from those who constantly fail or produce only mediocre results? What do you think are ten habits of successful people? Write out your ideas.

The Science of Goal Engineering

"Patience, persistence and perspiration make an unbeatable combination for success."

— Napoleon Hill

Goals forge powerful roots that build toward long-lasting success and achievement. A system of motivating goals, supported by a commitment to a consistent plan of action, is part of the formula that drives people to succeed.

Creating a system of goals that excite you adds incredible value to your life. A big goal constructs the building blocks for a prosperous future. By creating a system of goals that inspire and motivate us to engage in positive action, we plant the roots of success and design a system that expands on every opportunity.

Goals have the power to unleash your greatest desires and aspirations. With these tools, you can reinforce the vision you have for the life you want to build. All things are possible as soon as you have decided on the course of action that must be taken.

As Lewis Carroll stated, "If you don't know where you're going, you'll probably end up somewhere else."

Your goals provide you with a sense of direction and are the blueprints to construct the reality of your dreams.

Goals provide clarity. Without a concise plan, we shift from one idea to the next. Our dreams become lofty prospects that never materialize into anything concrete. Once you know where you are going, it is much easier to reach your destination when you have a clear line of sight ahead, driven by a system of progressive steps to get you there.

Getting the Details Right

In its most basic form, a goal is a unit of measurement—your own personal success meter—that tells you how far you have come and the distance to your destination. To have your goals eventually materialize as tangibles in the real world, you must know precisely what you want.

This is achieved when you approach your goals as a creative visionary and by integrating as much detail as possible into your plan.

If you want to build a new home, figure out as many of the details as you can. How does it look from the outside? What is the exact size and model? Where is it located? How many rooms are there, and what does it look like inside? Is there a garden in front? What color is it? Is it made of brick or stucco? Does it have a Jacuzzi or a sauna? Does it have a hobby room or workspace?

Detail builds reality. It moves you from a dreamer to a believer. What the mind can see, it will achieve.

Immediately follow through with a concrete plan that takes you from A to Z. First, build the details in your mind with absolute accuracy. This will give you an incredible insight by helping you to focus on the right actions needed to get where you want to be.

Identifying and being specific about exactly what you want enhances your vision and makes it all the more real. From building a new home to writing a book, taking a trip around the world or designing a new product for your company, everything begins with an idea. This molds the future and the vision becomes reality.

When you know what you want, the journey becomes more real. Being explicit in what you are setting out to achieve makes a difference between following a well-detailed map with all the roads and places labeled and just following a simple drawing with vague directions.

The Steps to Creating Goals

"By recording your dreams and goals on paper, you set in motion the process of becoming the person you most want to be. Put your future in good hands—your own."

— Mark Victor Hansen

Now that we know what is possible, it's time to begin the work that will establish your course of action with greater focus.

It's time to write down your goals. Once this step is done, you will be able to identify the work that needs to be completed so your future vision will be realized. To keep this simple, I have broken the process up to cover fourteen days.

Yes, within fourteen days you will have completed a goal portfolio. Does this seem impossible or hard to believe? If so, it's because this may be your first time trying this.

Now, I recommend setting aside a minimum of thirty minutes a day until all the steps are completed. Follow the steps below to create your personal profile of custom goals designed to build success in the essential areas of your life.

Day 1 / Create Goal Categories

In Word, Google Docs or your notebook, use individual pages to write the following ten categories at the top of the page. If you need more categories that are more customized to your goals, feel free to add them. Goal categories:

- Career and Business
- Family/Child Development/Spousal Relationship
- Hobbies and Special Interests
- Education/Specialized Training
- Travel

- Financial/Savings/Investment/Retirement
- Volunteerism
- Personal Development
- Health, Fitness, and Lifestyle

If there are any other categories you would like to add that are not already listed, you can do that now.

Total Time: 20 minutes

Days 2 and 3 / Mind-Mapping Your Ideas

Under each heading, mind map as many goals as you can for each individual category. Spend 10 to 15 minutes on each category. Mind map all the ideas, hopes, and dreams you have ever had within each particular area of your life.

For example, your Career and Business Goals may look like this:

1. Get my business management degree.
2. Quit my current job and take something better.
3. Start my own internet business within five years.

Write down as many ideas as you can. You will be working out the details later.

Don't worry about how or when you are going to do this just yet. The key is to get everything in your head down on paper so you can physically see it.

Note: One or two of your categories will probably dominate the others, depending on the concentration of your interests. This is good. You don't want to focus on everything, but just two to three areas will be your primary goals.

Day 4 / Prioritizing

Next, go back and read through the goals you have listed for each category. Number the goals from the most important (power goals) to the least important (important, but not urgent). Prioritizing what needs to be done first is a vital step to building momentum in your daily actions.

For example, if your goal is to run a full marathon, you have to be able to run a half-marathon before you can do the full one. Your goals are achieved by "step building" or doing things in order by following a certain process. Your goal, depending on how many stages there are, may involve twenty individual actions. You have to identify which actions you need to take and when.

Day 5 / Create a Power Goals List

On a separate sheet of paper, write "My Power Goals" at the top of the page. This is for priority goals. These are the dominant objectives in each of your categories, since achieving a power goal would have a significant impact on your life. Take from each category one goal you listed as the most important and cluster them in this section.

Then, tack this list up where you can see it. You want to have a constant reminder of what your power goals are so that you can stay focused on working towards them. You may decide to work on just one at a time, or work on two goals simultaneously. I recommend staying focused on your biggest impact goal as a priority and using other goals to support this.

Day 6 / Set Out Power Goals

Next, assign a separate sheet of paper to each of the power goals. Write the power goal at the top of the page. For example, if one power goal is "Travel across Europe," this is what I will write at the top of the page.

According to the nine categories above, if you had a power goal for each one, you would then need nine separate pages for each power goal. Later on, you will write down a list of actions under each power goal heading.

Day 7 / Establish a Master Goal

Select the goal that would have the greatest impact on your life from your list of power goals. This is a goal that could boost your quality of life, make a dramatic change, or raise the bar on everything you are involved in.

This is your master goal, your center of concentration, and the foundation for everything else. In your notebook, write this master goal at the top of the page. Later, you will create a set of short- and long-term action steps to get you moving on this. Now select your master goal and write it down.

Note: The master goal is what I consider the ultimate goal. If you accomplish it, it would have a major impact on your life. I call it the "Groundbreaker Goal," and it represents the cornerstone of all your dreams.

> "All who have accomplished great things have had a great aim, have fixed their gaze on a goal which was high, one which sometimes seemed impossible."
>
> — Orison Swett Marden

Day 8 / Create a Compelling Reason for Each Goal

Before you begin any new venture, you should first create a compelling reason for your actions. This simple task puts your goal in perspective. Answering and confirming the reasons why something is important gives the desire a life of its own.

Why does this goal matter to you? How will accomplishing this goal have a positive impact on your life? What would happen if you did not accomplish it?

Create compelling reasons for each of your goals. Write down your answers to these questions.

Day 9 / The Action Plan

What are the action steps you must take for each of your power goals? Remember that a goal is achieved through following a specific plan of action. Just saying that you want to do something is not enough—you must take the action necessary to build the momentum that gets things moving in the right direction.

In this next step, for each of your power goals, I want you to write a bulleted list of the steps you can take to begin working on each goal. In some cases, it might be as simple as making a phone call to gather information, filling out an application, or applying for a loan at the bank. This is the development of your master plan for each power goal.

Day 10 / Make a Deadline

What is the deadline for your goals? I have goals that have taken five years to complete. Others took only a few weeks. Another power goal has taken over ten years and is still ongoing.

Whatever it is you desire to achieve, set a specific completion date. Make sure the date is realistic and achievable. If it isn't, you will find yourself resetting it, again and again, every time you miss the deadline.

Once you have set your target date, set daily and weekly goals (your power steps) that move you closer to your target date. With each step completed, you will be moving closer to finishing it.

For short-term goals, your deadline may be in a matter of weeks or months. If it is a long-term goal, you can set the year and the month. For example, "I will have achieved this goal by December of next year."

Day 11 / Review

Now go back and read through each of your power goals. This step is meant to review what you have designed so far. I want you to choose the top three goals from your list of power goals and focus mainly on these. I am not suggesting ignoring the other goals.

However, if you try to do too much you will end up with nothing. Decide which goals are most important and will contribute the most to designing your life the way you envisioned it to be.

Choose the top three and spend ten minutes a day visualizing the final outcome of these goals. Post these goals up where you can see them every morning when you wake up and again before you go to bed. Plan your action steps at the start of every week for each of your priority goals. Be consistent in taking your action steps.

Day 12 / Building the Vision

Visualization is a big part of making our dreams come true. For the next two days, I want you to think about your goals. Visualize yourself working toward them. See yourself overcoming the obstacles that block your success.

Imagine what it will feel like when you have achieved your victory. Spend some time mentally conditioning yourself for success. Imagine your goals have already been achieved and piece together the visionary puzzle that will put you in the right frame of mind.

Nothing happens without first imagining it as being so. Make it real in your mind and it will eventually become your reality. Now, write your vision down in as much detail as possible. This is to be a visual letter to yourself. Before you visualize each day, read over your visual letter at least twice.

Day 13 / Identify Your Achilles' Heel

Everyone has weaknesses, or at least one potentially threatening weakness that stands out amongst the rest. It is this weakness that could be holding you back from achieving your maximum potential and fulfilling your goals. This could be a negative habit, or the lack of some specific knowledge or skill you have to acquire before any progress can be made.

In most cases, failure to reach your goals is the result of an internal weakness that you have failed to address. Take a look at the goals you have written down. For each one, make a note of any obstacles or personal defects that need to be overcome in order for you to succeed.

By identifying your "Achilles' heel," you will be able to transform your most prominent weakness into your greatest strength.

What obstacles do you see holding you back? How can you work through this roadblock and succeed? Identify two people who can help you with this? Knowing where you are weakest is an attribute because you can mend what needs to be healed.

Day 14 / Acquire the Necessary Skills, Connections, or Knowledge

Goals don't just happen by chance. The accomplishment of your life's dream is the combination of many other steps in between. This includes acquiring new skills or techniques you need in order to move forward with your plan.

If your goal is to take part in a triathlon, you might have to become a stronger swimmer, in which case swimming lessons could be necessary. If you have a great idea for a small business but you lack business knowledge and experience, you might consider taking a small business course, or interviewing people who are already running their own companies.

Regardless of your lack of expertise, knowledge or experience, anything is possible if you are willing to put in the time and effort. Remember, no matter what you are trying to do, in most cases there is someone out there that can help you succeed. Try to make the right connections and relationships with the people who can give you the advice or know-how necessary to succeed.

Now, for each of your goals, identify the skills or specialized knowledge you need to succeed. Is it a book you have to read to acquire knowledge? An interview with someone who has already succeeded in what you are trying to do? A course you have to take?

Make a list of the necessary skills you need and the people you must connect with in order to bring you closer to meeting your goals.

The Weekly Review

The most important step for managing your goals is committing to a weekly review of your goals. By performing the review phase every week, you will be able to maintain a level of organized functionality as you identify the current actions being taken and those actions or steps that have to be taken next.

Through the review phase, you will create a system of measurement with which you can keep track of what has been done, what hasn't been done, what needs to be modified, and what needs to be done next.

The review process puts everything in perspective. It allows you freedom and opportunity to analyze, interpret, and plan for the next course of action. Instead of just plunging ahead day by day, doing whatever comes to your mind in a haphazard order, the weekly review allows you to observe yourself as you work.

This provides you with the opportunity to look for areas that need more attention. It keeps you focused on important matters so you don't become distracted.

I recommend setting aside a thirty-minute block of time each week, either at the beginning of the week or the end. In this session, do the following:

1. Check off the sub-goals and actions completed this week.
2. Make a note of those actions that were not completed and move them to next week.
3. Confirm your goals and sub-goals for the week. Make a list of actions to be taken or tasks to be done and place it in a visible or easily accessible spot.
4. Read over your mission statement or master goal.
5. Put any important dates, appointments, or deadlines on your wall calendar.
6. Take time to organize or clean up any loose ends that could become distracting. Stay organized.

7. Review your goals from all categories. Even if most of these goals are things you want to do in the distant future, it is always a good idea to keep them fresh in your mind.
8. Write out any additional ideas or thoughts you had during the week. Add any new goals to your list.
9. Take 20 to 30 minutes at the end to visualize your outcome.

Review your goal progress once a week and check off the completed tasks. Make it a habit to end each week with a review of your goals. This is a vital step for tracking your progress.

How to Reverse Engineer the Next Ten Years

Now that you have a list of goals, I want to introduce you to a fantastic way to set the rest of your life up for success. Many people either don't have goals, or they work on their goals for a few months without much progress. It takes time to achieve big goals that could possibly change your life.

One challenge people have is that they struggle to define how this goal will positively impact their lives. What started as something fun and exciting soon became a burden. To best maximize your success at finishing your goals, use the reverse engineering strategy. It is also referred to as the "beginning with the end in mind," and Stephen Covey discusses this in his bestselling book, The 7 Habits of Highly Effective People.

This is how it works:

Visualize your life in the next twenty years. Or if that is too far ahead, you can scale back to ten years. See yourself living your life the way you want. Block in twenty minutes a day for this exercise. You can use the Pomodoro timer app to stay focused.

Now, consider these questions when practicing visualization:

Where are you in ten years? Who are you with? How do you spend your days? Do you wake up each morning with a renewed enthusiasm for living, or are you dragging yourself out of bed every morning to go to a job you hate?

Have you found someone to share the rest of your life with? Are you still struggling financially, or are you doing well because you have achieved your goals? Who have you helped along the way? What are people saying about you when you're not around? How has your life developed in the past ten years because you set out to make things happen with hard work and commitment?

This form of future visualizing is powerful. In my opinion, without this practice, you will get to the point where you feel stuck. You may lose confidence. Uncertainty might settle in. You start to question whether you're doing the right thing or if you will ever succeed.

I can tell you without a doubt that every successful person has moments of doubt, uncertainty, and fears. But we can transcend these fearful thoughts by projecting the way we want the story to end.

It can feel as if we're moving through each day guessing how the end will turn out. Have you ever asked people whether they have a plan for the future, and they responded by saying, "I don't know—I'll just see how it works out"?

Well, I can't predict my future but I can visualize how I want it to turn out, and I can take the right actions today to get me to where I want to be in five, ten, twenty years from now. Can you take five minutes right now to put your imagination to work and throw your thoughts into the future?

> "The mystery of human existence lies not in just staying alive, but in finding something to live for."
>
> — Fyodor Dostoyevsky

Once you have a clear picture of yourself exactly where you want to be emotionally, mentally, and physically, happier than you've ever been, ask yourself this:

What actions did I take to get there?

A goal without massive action is called a dream, and a lofty dream at best. You want to do more than just dream about what life could be like. You want to experience it and be the person you always wanted to be. Or maybe this is the first time you've actually given it any thought. Well, start now.

Work backward from the end and see yourself taking action every day.

What habits did you develop? Did you make a daily task list and work from that? Who did you seek for guidance? What lessons did you learn along the way? How did you overcome fear and get through tough obstacles?

By seeing yourself take action and visualizing the results, you will gain clarity on the necessary steps.

For example, let's say that one of your goals is to attain financial freedom. We know from experience that people who save cash and build a financial nest egg do so by planning ahead. Or they hired someone to do the planning for them.

Either way, if I wanted to save $30,000 in the next ten years, I could break it down to a monthly goal. To save this much money, I'd need to put away $300 a month. To achieve that, I could save $10 a day. How would I save $10 a day?

Now, this is where the action steps come into play. Not everyone has ten dollars a day to put away. But how much could you save by cutting back on expenses? Do you go to Starbucks every day? Do you spend more than twenty bucks a week on alcohol or smoking? You may have to cut back on your expenses.

This would require diligence and holding on to that vision of being financially free in ten years. If you wanted to do it in five, do the math and adjust accordingly.

You can do this for any goal. Start at the end and work your way back through all of the action steps required.

If you want to learn how to play the piano in a year, how much practice would you put in every week?

If you want to write a book, how many words would you write every day until finished?

Some goals will be long-term and others short-term, but your goals can cross over and support each other. If want to save $30,000 within ten years, but cash is tight, you could try writing a book or a series of books and create a platform. If you market and advertise and build a following, you now have additional income.

The reverse engineering process is the most logical way to get your goals done and will drive you to persevere even when times are difficult.

Here are the steps for reverse engineering your life:

1. Visualize your life 10 to 20 years from now. How are you living? Who have you become by accomplishing your dream?
2. Visually walk back through your life and work out the action steps needed to take you from here to there.
3. Break your action steps down into manageable chunks. You want this action plan to be realistic and achievable. While saving $30,000 is overwhelming, saving $5 a day is manageable and possible.
4. Create sustainable habits along the way. Your daily routine and habits will assure that you are hitting your daily mini-goals.

Spend 10 minutes every night visualizing your future as it will be in 20 years. This keeps your motivation at its peak and makes the dream real.

Action Plan

1. Choose one important goal from your list of goals and start working on it right away. Create a list of action tasks that you have to complete in order to achieve this goal. Then, work on this until you reach your goal. Focus on nothing else except finishing.

2. Review your progress at the end of each day or week and create a set of daily and weekly tasks to do at the beginning of every new week. You can set monthly goals as well and break it down into your weekly and daily goals.

3. In twenty years, where do you see yourself? What kind of person have you developed into because of the success you have achieved? Write down your ideas.

4. Set a timer for thirty minutes. In this time, make a list of twenty goals you would like to achieve in your lifetime. You don't have to add any specific details or a deadline at this time. Once you finish, go back later and select the ten most important goals. Using the process above, create a list of action steps you would have to take to accomplish this goal.

The Window of Opportunity

"What happened yesterday is history. What happens tomorrow is a mystery. What we do today makes a difference - the precious present moment."

— Nick Saban

It is never too late to pursue and reach your goals. It is never too late to embrace the life you desire to live. It is never too late to go back to school, make new friends, or engage in a new business practice.

It is never too late to find love or discover the endless love within your own heart, and it is never too late to seize opportunity or take a risk on something you have spent your life avoiding.

In fact, it is never too late for anything. You can do whatever you desire if you have determination to pursue life's bountiful treasures.

This world is in a state of constant change. New chances are created every day. In today's world of rapidly evolving information, ideas and technology, it seems the world is thriving with more opportunity than ever before. New pathways to success are being created all the time.

As the world evolves and changes from day to day, our choices and opportunities change with it. What was available to you yesterday may be a closed deal today as someone else has already moved in and seized the chance that you declined. You may regret some of the opportunities you passed up years ago but dwelling on what you lost only creates more of the same.

Regardless of what you have gained or lost in the past, there are still many chances to be successful in work and all other aspects of life. Knowing this truth is a revelation that inspires hope.

An opportunity that was lost ages ago could be rejuvenated years later in a different form. As the world changes and expands, people and countries come closer together and economies merge, our opportunity for advancement has never been greater. The key is to know what you want and to watch for those chances when they appear.

Seize the Moment

I first became aware of the window of opportunity years ago when I had to accept the painful truth that one of my lifelong dreams was probably never going to happen. It was just too late. My dream would always be just a dream. No matter how hard I worked at it, it was likely it would never come true. I had missed my window of opportunity.

Suddenly I became aware of the concept of time and how, every year, that window of opportunity was slowly closing all around me. Either I was too old to achieve my dreams, or the circumstances that I had ten years ago had changed so drastically that what I wanted became impossible to pursue.

The window of opportunity I thought would always be there had become outdated and closed for good.

There is a limited timeframe for every opportunity that exists. This window is only open for a brief moment and then it's gone entirely. For children, this window remains wide open with unlimited potential as new talents and skills are acquired and the child's interest in various subjects is quickly recognized.

A child may take a risk or try something new and unique without realizing it. In time, however, the risks taken become fewer. Fear or reason stand in the way to block you from moving on a once-in-a-lifetime opportunity. Those who take risks might lose. And yet, those who don't act at all will certainly lose.

Some people create opportunity where there is none. Others destroy it or fail to take action on account of letting fear stand in the way. Like a great tsunami that destroys all in its wake, we are in competition with the window of time as it slowly draws closed before we can seize life's prospects.

In order to take advantage of the many opportunities surrounding you, you have to have a solid idea of what you are looking for. If not, every idea and every opportunity looks like a good one. You might end up chasing the wrong dream if you don't know what you really need.

You need to know beforehand what you are searching. When the chance presents itself, you won't have to question whether it's the right one. You will know intuitively that this opportunity was created for you. If you wander aimlessly without any clue as to what you want, you will fail to recognize that chance when it comes knocking at your door.

Stay in touch with things you feel passionate about. Keep your interests alive and stay focused on areas that make a difference to the quality of your life. Do not get caught up in small activities or petty trifles that distract your concentration. When you are focused in on what matters, you are in a strong position to create your opportunity, or you will be ready for it when the time comes.

The key is to know when to act and take action when an opportunity feels right. Don't be afraid to take an acceptable risk but weigh the situation carefully if you have to. If you hesitate because of fear, the opportunity will be lost and become another's profit.

In situations like this, people often say, "Oh, don't worry, another opportunity will come by."

Maybe it will and maybe it won't. If you're stranded in the middle of the ocean, you can't always be fussy about every passing ship.

Window of Unlimited Abundance

Imagine there's an open window in your mind. This window is large enough that anything you desire could fit through it—a job offer, a chance to buy a new home, or a lucrative investment deal with the possibility of making you a fortune in just a few years.

Through this window is where all of life's prospects, lucrative offers, and unlimited opportunities are ready to come pouring through each day. Imagine that everything you have ever desired is flowing through this window of opportunity in endless abundance.

Now, you can't seize everything, but you can seize the opportunity you want the most. As I mentioned already, the key is in knowing what you're looking for.

Which opportunity best serves your present needs and fulfills the purpose and vision of your life? Without knowing what you want, the chance of a lifetime could be staring you in the face and you might walk right past it. If you could have anything, what would it be? If any choice were available to you, what would it be? What is the chance you are seeking that hasn't appeared yet?

When it feels right, there is no hesitation. Your intuition will serve you well in the moment when your greatest opportunity approaches.

Life is bountiful when you believe the abundance of opportunity you seek is all around you. If you believe your choices in this world are limited and confined, then this is the reality you will experience. You will never find what you are looking for if you think everything happens by mere luck or coincidence.

You are in a position right now to create the opportunity you desire. There has to be a set of actions beforehand: a decision, a proposal, or an action that produces significant results. When you just wait for things to happen, you leave yourself at the mercy of outside forces and no longer control the events directing your life.

When the opportunity you want is not available, you don't have to sit around and wait for it to happen. Keep moving and keep working. Keep dreaming and keep trying. Be selective in your choices and decisive with your actions. You can have anything you want but be sure it's the one thing you desire more than anything.

You have to let go of regrets. Missed opportunities will never return, at least not in the same form. Regretting lost opportunity quickly dissolves the abundance of new prospects. Do not regress. Stick with what you have today. When opportunity fails to knock, build your own doors and invite success in.

The future is in this moment right now, and it is built through actions and choices that generate the opportunity you seek. You have to know what you're going after so you can recognize the opportunity when it appears.

Time is Opportunity

Thomas Edison, who achieved so much in his lifetime, and with over 1,000 recognized patents, utilized the same amount of time that you have right now.

Stephen King, who has been an international best-selling author for more than forty years, has written over sixty novels, many of them worldwide bestsellers.

It is estimated that Pablo Picasso produced over 50,000 artworks during his time, including paintings, ceramics and sculptures.

How can the world's super-achievers accomplish more in a week than many people can in a year? What separates a world-class inventor, writer, or artist from everyone else? Are they smarter, wiser, or funnier? Were they born into good fortune? Do they have more time?

The days are still twenty-four hours long, yet most of us can barely scratch the surface of what we hope to accomplish. How did Thomas Edison do it? Well, Thomas Edison knew how to manage time. He was also driven by his passions.

This fueled his desire to work long hours. He created his own world of opportunity by following his passions and applying a willingness to work more than the average person. While most would give up, he pushed on. And for people with this level of persistence, their chances of succeeding are exponential. Edison didn't wait for his chance. He seized it over and over again.

"Most people miss opportunity because it is dressed in overalls and looks like work."

— Thomas A. Edison

The key is to know what to do and when to do it. You know you have two free hours ahead of you this evening. How you decide to spend them is up to you. If you have a passion for doing something, you have to make the time for it. If you wait until you are completely free or the time is just right, you might never get around to it.

A friend of mine is a novelist. He writes ten pages a day, yet he has four kids, a family, and another job, but still he writes ten pages a day. That is because writing those pages is one of the most important things in his day. He simply knows that he must do this every day.

That is the sacrifice and the discipline. While others are at home watching TV or out drinking every weekend, he is at home every night writing his next novel. He creates his own opportunity in life by taking action and knowing what he wants.

Knowing what you want to do, when to do it, and by putting yourself into action mode in order to achieve it opens that window of opportunity a little wider, regardless of age, social status or education. If the opportunity you desire doesn't come knocking, go out and look for it.

You have to pursue it with a relentless obsession in order to seize it and make it yours. In other words, the individual who waits around for success is wasting time. The people who take action and refuse to give up achieve their dreams.

While I lost several opportunities over the years, this didn't mean everything was over. I created new choices. I made new goals and pursued opportunities. You can do the same, regardless of what's passed you by. There will never be a shortage of opportunity, only a lack of imagination.

Be an Opportunity-Minded Individual

We waste too much energy and scarce resources waiting for empty opportunities that never materialize, meanwhile forgetting that the best chance we have of succeeding is to be the opportunity you want to have.

You are the best chance at success you will ever discover. Think about it. Nobody else is like you, and that means you are unique. Failing to take advantage of your own opportunity is like sitting on top of a mountain of gold without realizing it, crying because you are broke and have no money.

Look inside yourself for the opportunity you want. What can you do that others can't? What do you excel in that others don't? What is different about you that makes you unique? In the end, there is only one person who will make the life you want, and that is you. Nobody knows you like you know yourself and only you will know when it's time to take advantage of that special opportunity.

Do you remember the old adage, "If it is too good to be true, it probably is"? Well, these thoughts have hung around for decades, and as we learn them, we believe in the self-defeating message they carry.

Have you ever approached someone with an offer that was considered reasonable only to have them reject you? How many times have people tried to convince you to take a risk on something that just seemed too easy?

We have been conditioned to be wary of opportunities that sound too good to be true. Opportunity is all around you. The problem is we don't always see it because we are too busy focusing on the sure thing that won't let us down. We continue to repeat our past failures by behaving and thinking the same way every day. This is how opportunity is lost.

A person with an open mind who is willing to take a chance on something has a significantly greater chance of succeeding than the person who does nothing. If you stand by and watch while others swoop in to seize those golden opportunities, their reward will be your loss. I am not suggesting you grab hold of every opportunity, but you do have a limited amount of time to think things through. Don't get caught up in imagining what the results may or may not be.

Most people fail to jump at something because they want a guarantee that things will work out, that they won't lose money or be humiliated in some way if the risk goes sour. Nobody can guarantee any opportunity is golden. The one thing that is guaranteed is that you will gain nothing if you do nothing.

> "It's not the lack of resources, it's your lack of resourcefulness that stops you."
>
> — Tony Robbins

When Ray Kroc purchased the McDonald's business from the McDonald brothers, they were invited to join him in a joint venture. They were given the opportunity to make a fortune and they didn't take it. They settled for 2.7 million, took the money, and Ray took the McDonald name and amassed a fortune that the brothers were never involved with.

Ray Kroc seized an opportunity to expand and build an empire. Those he approached later on, to help expand on the opportunity, were later rewarded with wealth, success, and lifelong careers.

Be wary of the negative consequences of the quick rejection phase that we learn at a young age. Be open-minded and cultivate the attitude that opportunity is all around you, and that you are right now searching for and keeping an open eye on the one golden opportunity that can change everything. People who are closed to opportunity are also closed to change and personal growth, two key ingredients necessary for attracting wealthy opportunity and choices.

Five Ways to Attract Greater Opportunity

"To hell with circumstances; I create opportunities."

— Bruce Lee

Sometimes opportunity happens by chance, but in many cases, the expectations we build draw it toward us. As a proactive person, you need to go after it, be ready for it, and know what to do when the time is right.

If you want to connect with the vast world of opportunity available, then you must become the kind of person who attracts the opportunity you desire. There are several ways to do this:

Know precisely what you want

When you know what you want, and you are able to visualize it, the opportunity you seek will present itself. This could be in the form of a new job offer, a chance encounter, or being in the right place at the right time with the right frame of mind that recognizes the chance when it appears.

It is much easier to be successful when you know what kind of success you want to attract. The opportunity you seek might involve a person you meet at just the right moment or something you needed desperately but didn't have before that has suddenly found its way into your life.

The universe has your best interests at heart and it is looking out for you. Be the kind of person you want to measure up to and the opportunity you desire has a high probability of appearing.

Trust yourself.

The most difficult part of this process is being able to trust yourself. People are afraid of making mistakes, of being lied to or cheated, and so a golden opportunity might be misperceived as a threat and disregarded.

But if you have a clear understanding of what your own intentions are and you know the direction in which you want to go, the laws of the universe will respond by providing you with the right opportunity.

Trust who you are, trust what you want and, most of all, trust that it is being delivered to you through your relationships and the pathways each new encounter presents.

Meet new people and expand on your relationships.

Meeting new people is one of the best ways to expand good fortune in life. By connecting and forming lasting bonds, you become rich in friendship, both personal and business. This creates new bridges of opportunity.

The more people you meet and connect with, the larger and richer your world grows. This brings more chances for opportunity to grow. With each new relationship you forge, your social presence is expanded.

With the reach of the Internet and high-powered social networks, never has there been more opportunity to meet new people. Take advantage of this and start to connect with those who add value to your life. Share your richness of life with them. In business or friendship, the quality of your relationships brings an unlimited wealth of abundance.

Every new friendship expands your global circle. Making new business contacts puts you in touch with people from various business cultures and backgrounds. Every new contact adds to a wealth of possibilities. Every new bond expands your chances for attracting opportunities and engaging in new friendships across the globe.

Learn something new.

Picking up new skills is a great way to expand upon your opportunity. If you are looking to start something new, it can be very difficult. You may have gone as far as you can in your current position because the skills and knowledge you have are outdated. If you want to expand new pathways, one of the best ways to do this is to create a new set of skills. Get educated in something different. Make yourself more marketable.

I know people who have created entirely new careers by learning another language, taking advanced computer courses, or getting an MBA. Once they had the skills, they were in a position to seek opportunity needed to advance beyond what they were accustomed to. These opportunities are available to anyone, but first we have to boost our knowledge or advance our skills to make an approachable offer.

Take that first step.

Decide what you want and make a list of the opportunities available to you. There are some things you can do right now to begin working on your plans for the future. If you wait for someday, there will be no more room for excuses.

You have to take advantage of the time you have left. Plan your day by putting together a list of action items for this week. Take a look at the opportunity that each of your actions could create.

Ask yourself, "Am I waiting for the perfect opportunity while the most important opportunities are passing me by? Is the window of opportunity going to close, or can it wait?"

There are some things that can or must wait, and there are those rare opportunities that must be snatched up before they are gone forever. Decide what your real talent is and work toward fulfilling those passions.

You have to be aware of what's calling to you right now. Is it something that requires your immediate action? If you find something you really want, don't let it slip away.

Seize that one critical moment. Get busy and get moving. Don't let a good thing go because you fear making the wrong decision. The graveyard of lost dreams is full of the sad stories about those who failed to act.

Adopting a Model
for Success

"There is no use whatsoever trying to help people who do not help themselves. You cannot push anyone up a ladder unless he is willing to climb himself."

— Andrew Carnegie

When we adopt the habits, techniques, and specific actions of successful achievers, we can create a similar model for success. By modeling the traits of successful people in sports, arts, music, or keynote speakers, you will experience a massive shift in the course your life is taking.

In essence, you become just like the people you spend the most time with. This includes modeling the strategies of others to push ahead and take your life to the next level.

Consider these questions:

1. If you could adopt the traits, values, and characteristics of the person you admire and respect the most for just one day, who would it be?

2. Would you model an influential politician, a motivational speaker, or a wise spiritual leader? Would it be a celebrity? How about a business entrepreneur?

3. What are the principles and values you admire the most in the people you desire to emulate? Is it their adherence to self-discipline? Is it an unwavering dedication to a noble cause? Is it a strong commitment to achieving excellence? Is it their kindness and generosity?

4. Is your ideal role model changing the way you perceive the world? Does he or she inspire and motivate others?

5. What unique traits do they possess that you would like to develop?

6. Do their actions, choices, and personal beliefs reflect the way you want to start living your life?

If you take the time to think carefully about your answers to these questions, you should have a good idea of who you desire to emulate. Now think about the specific areas of your life that you would need to develop to get you there.

By seeking someone to become your coach, mentor or guide, someone who has similar goals, you can walk the journey together to experience the joys of living.

The need to adopt a model for success in our lives has never been greater. When you choose a mentor or role model, by modeling the traits that make them high-level achievers, the same core dynamics and opportunity that builds their success becomes readily available to you.

Setting Personal Standards

When you adopt a model for success, you are setting the standards by which you want to succeed. These standards define you and everything you want to represent. Your most suitable role model will be the person who represents your best interests. Everything they say and do should reflect the way you desire to think, act, and behave.

Change begins with a desire to transition ourselves from one state to another, and from one mindset to another. Having a good role model can result in their habits becoming your habits, their thoughts influencing your thoughts.

Most importantly, the positive values and traits of your role models could become your own if you listen, observe, and adopt similar behaviors. Recruiting the right mentor will create a lasting and binding relationship, filled with positive energy, personal empowerment, and a life of greater fulfillment and satisfaction.

You may be thinking, "But why would I want to become just like someone else? I'm happy with who I am."

The goal is not to turn yourself into a carbon copy of another person. Your uniqueness plays a vital role in defining you as an individual. But, when we model the way successful people think and behave, we start to transform our own lives.

The values and principles you adopt from your role model can be added to your personality to enhance your character, enabling you to evolve in the next stage of your journey. Your values and characteristics define your character. They become a part of you as you train yourself to think, do, and behave differently.

When we do things differently with intention, real change is converted into powerful results. Instead of living by default, we switch this over to a life driven by intentional choices. When this is followed by taking massive action, you find yourself doing the things you once only imagined.

In today's world, you can seek out models for success just about everywhere. Your role models could be people in your schools, places of business or those who live right in our communities. They could be teachers and parents, police and firefighters, business entrepreneurs and restaurant owners, living right in your community.

They don't have to be famous or rich or have any kind of celebrity status. They could be ordinary people with extraordinary gifts who want to share what they have with you, your family, and the global community.

Six Qualities of a Good Role Model

> "We should be inspired by people... who show that human beings can be kind, brave, generous, beautiful, strong-even in the most difficult circumstances."
>
> — Rachel Corrie

A good role model should meet certain criteria. The principles and values you look for in a mentor depend heavily on the context of your vision and objectives. In other words, the role model you are drawn to may be someone who walked a similar path, maybe in the same industry as you, or shares a set of beliefs that are similar to yours. All leaders share similar core qualities.

A good role model inspires others to reach their full potential.

A good role model is an influential force in this world. They are positive thinkers. The actions and words they live by encourage others to do the same. The strength of these positive words and actions are passed down through generations.

When people are passionate and inspired, they feel compelled to teach others what they know.

Today, there is a movement of people who are looking beyond just gathering material goods or making more money. They want to experience life at a deeper level through a deeper satisfaction in their jobs, building stronger personal relationships, and expanding on spiritual knowledge and personal development. A role model or mentor who delivers effective encouragement goes a long way in making people feel appreciated.

A good role model overcomes obstacles and difficulties.

Positive role models face their fears and overcome problems and obstacles by working out the best solutions. Today's commercialism and advertising are influencing people to take the easy way out to become happy and successful.

By adopting and integrating the same values that are upheld by a good role model, you can learn that success is only possible when you have confronted your fears. Learning to cope with and overcome difficult challenges is a critical step to building lasting confidence.

Once you commit to making positive changes in your own life, you become more courageous and share this with others. Transitioning from self-serving ideas puts you in a position to be of greater service to others. A good role model shows you that being of service to other people is the highest point of living.

You can help by providing advice, solutions, or simply listening to problems and hardships. You may not be able to fix their problems, but you can certainly relieve their pain by being there and making yourself available.

Role models are global volunteers.

The best role models are those who volunteer out of service and volunteerism. Such role models could be celebrities and spiritual leaders, teachers and parents, political leaders and social workers. You can find such role models right in your own town, in the news, in books, and even in your immediate family.

Regardless of where you encounter them, read their stories and study what they do. Listen to their words of wisdom, confidence, and the message they convey. Subsequently, seek to support your own global concerns by getting involved. You can make a difference.

A role model is a visual creator and leader.

The greatest leaders in this world have a vision for the future and that vision is shared by anyone who embraces it as their own.

For example, if you are a parent and you serve as one of the role models for your children, you're creating a vision for them. A spiritual leader is concerned with the future of his disciples. The president of a country develops a vision for the nation. CEOs have a vision for their business. Teachers instruct students how to build a vision for the future they want to create.

What is your vision? Is there a leader or role model whose vision you are paying attention to? Visionaries are masters at creating the future by teaching others the best actions they can take to support one another.

A role model lives by a set of well-defined principles and values.

A person is defined by their principles and values. Successful people are aware of the values that drive them. They are also committed to a set of principles that define their actions.

Strong leaders have a set of principles and values that act as the foundation of all their actions. Your principles and values are the rules and guidelines that form the basis for all your actions.

A role model creates leaders.

One of the key characteristics of role models and leaders is the ability to create other role models and leaders. When you adopt the values and characteristics of a well-defined leader, you take on the responsibility of becoming a leader yourself. You then have a responsibility to pass on what you have learned to future generations.

It is the role of great leaders to teach others how to lead and not just follow. A role model wants you to think for yourself and come to your own conclusions. Embracing your own confidence and making key decisions are signs that you are moving on and growing.

Adopting a Role Model
for Success

"Setting an example is not the main means of influencing others; it is the only means."

— Albert Einstein

In addition to the core qualities of role models previously mentioned, here are five basic guidelines for seeking out your models.

Identify the type of model you want to emulate.

Write down the areas of your life you want to improve, expand, and develop. Then make a list of potential role models that could help you move toward more success.

Gathering as much knowledge as possible about the characteristics of a role model will provide you with powerful insight into their core beliefs and personal values. Write down the values and principles that your ideal role model lives by. Then seek to integrate these principles into your life.

An example might be:

- Insightful
- Open-minded
- Passionate
- Wise
- Cultivated vision
- Diligent
- Disciplined
- Considerate and thoughtful

Choose a role model who has gained the level of success you want to achieve.

Several years ago, I made a list of role models I wanted to emulate based on their contributions to the world, values, and consistent habits and actions that defined who they are. Not all of these people were accessible to me, but I could learn about them by reading their books, listening to their tapes or podcasts, or following their daily blogs, while implementing methods they used.

We have a strong tendency to become like people we observe and emulate, so ensure you select people who are successful at the same things you want to do. Adopt their behaviors and learn to think like they do. When you do this, you will be taking the first steps toward personal transformation.

Identify the role models that fit your area of interest.

Identify at least three people who have achieved success in the same field. Is it in business, spirituality, or entertainment? Write down how you plan to gain access to their knowledge. Can you contact them?

Remember, a role model is not necessarily someone you have to meet and converse with personally. If you wish to adopt a role model for financial success, you could select a person who is an expert in this field and read their books or attend one of their seminars. Anyone who has achieved the level of success you endeavor to achieve qualifies as a model for success.

There is no limit to the number of people you can adopt as role models. I have a wide range of interests. Other than people who have the same set of principles as me, I model different individuals for financial organization, project management, self-discipline, and personal development.

I don't think there is any one person who can serve as a role model for all our interests. It is an effective strategy to adopt several role models to gain confidence and achieve success in every area of your life.

Identify the character traits of your role model.

Briefly describe all the character traits of your role model. Write down the reasons why this person is a solid choice for ensuring your success. Why are these character traits important to you?

From the list of character traits, identify traits and values you consider most important and strive to seek out role models who take actions according to these values. It is essential that you select a role model who has the character values you desire to adopt. A list of character traits is provided subsequently in this chapter.

Identify with your role model's impact on the community, country, and world.

Does the role model represent a certain group, set of ideals, or values that you admire? One way to seek out an effective role model is to consider their relationship with the world. Is this person well-respected or popular? Are they an influential figure with many followers?

Most leaders influence the world around them. Study their level of influence and decide if you would also like to have the same influence. Is this person a strong leader in your community? Does this role model influence world events? How has this person influenced you? How will you use this knowledge to influence others?

Creating a Character Traits List

Below is a list of core values to enable you to select your model for success. Choose the traits that are most important to you. I would recommend you select at least three values that you want to integrate into your life.

Subsequently, start looking for those values in the people you respect and admire. Adopt that person as a role model for both personal self-development and improving the quality of your life

Now make a list of the traits you want and seek to discover these character qualities in your role models. Remember, you can have more than one role model. I have had several and each individual contributed uniquely to my personal growth and development.

Surround yourself with a team of positive and inspiring people. Make it your goal to create a global alliance of positive role models.

Connecting with accomplished people enables you to become a role model yourself. There are no limits. Forging a powerful alliance with great men and women, who are focused and dedicated to making a difference, will significantly influence your life and the lives of those you meet.

Remember that every good deed is remembered and the changes you strive to implement today directly influence the world and everything in it.

Here is a list of positive character traits:

- High level of commitment
- High level of conscious awareness
- Empathy
- Integrity
- Humility
- Honesty
- Positive mental attitude
- Contribution and service
- Purpose in life
- Inspires and motivates through right action
- Responsible and reliable
- Insightful
- Open-minded
- Passionate
- Wise
- Cultivated vision
- Diligent
- Disciplined
- Considerate and thoughtful

- Emotionally and spiritually intelligent
- Respectful of others feelings and needs
- Successful and hardworking
- A sense of challenge and adventure
- Promotes self-efficacy
- Treats others as equal
- Encourages global relationships

When you seek out the people who are committed to building the future, you commit yourself to joining an alliance of global winners. Think deeply about those you desire to emulate and apply your energy to focusing on the person you want to become. Do everything you can to create the changes you have always wanted to integrate into your life and, most of all, remember you don't have to do it alone.

Action Plan

1. What kind of person is your ideal model for success? Briefly describe their traits and explain why this person is the best choice.

2. What changes would you have to make to rise to the same level? What new values would you have to integrate? What is the first step you can take to start making these changes today?

3. Do you want to become a role model? What actions would you take to achieve your own goals as a model of success for others? How would you inspire them?

4. Write about an influential role model who has made considerable changes to the world through their efforts. What values did they possess? What obstacles did they overcome? How did they influence the world? How does the rest of the world view this person?

The Power of
Priority Planning

"I learned that we can do anything, but we can't do everything
… at least not at the same time. So, think of your priorities, not
in terms of what activities you do, but when you do them.
Timing is everything."

— Dan Millman

Priority planning is the systematic organization and execution of primary tasks and activities directed toward achieving critical objectives and goals. By focusing on the high impact areas of your life first, you will become more efficient at organizing and managing your life.

This system of priority planning relates to putting what matters most at the top of the list. When you identify the key elements you need to focus on in any given situation, you will have set the precedent for your success in all worthy endeavors.

Regardless of whether you are trying to organize a family vacation, create a new product, or improve the working order of your office, when you follow a system of priority-focused tasks, supported by a detailed vision, the acquired results have tremendous potential to redirect the pathways of your life.

The journey you take to get there becomes a dynamic learning experience as you train yourself to concentrate on becoming victorious in those areas of your life that make the biggest difference.

By identifying with the work, tasks, and activities that capture your attention, you'll be able to determine what matters most and what needs to be done about it. You can then put together a list of action steps to support each task that leads to a successful outcome.

Here are some questions to consider:

- Do you need to spend less time at the office and more time with your family?
- Have you been focusing on the little stuff, while the big stuff goes neglected?
- Is there an unfinished project that has been sitting in a drawer somewhere that requires attention?
- Do you get caught up in things and find that, even after working a full day, you have achieved nothing?
- Are you easily pulled into other people's emergency situations?
- How much time and energy do you spend doing things for other people just to keep them content and happy? As a result, do you feel you have less time to take care of your own stuff?
- Do you have a list of organized tasks to perform each week? Are these actions in alignment with your goals and life purpose?
- What areas of interest capture your attention? Do you spend enough time in this area of your life?

Identify what matters the most to you and redirect your energy to concentrate on these areas of your life that have the potential to make the biggest difference. This could be comprised of unfinished work, an idea for a new project, or areas of your life you've neglected.

You can get started now by looking around at the unfinished work, disorganized office, or distractions that you spend too much time on.

Significant changes can only take place when you organize your thoughts and actions to focus on whatever has the most potential to add significant value. When you make a hard note of what matters the most, all the little stuff stealing your time and energy loses significance.

Focus your mental energy on making significant progress in the areas that give you the most return on your investment. A lack of focus results in poor choices.

Determining Your Priorities

Knowing your priorities is critical to staying focused. By concentrating on tasks that are in alignment with your present goals, you are laying down the foundation for developing a powerful support system that puts everything in perspective. If you lose focus on things that matter, you will fall prey to things that don't.

Priority planning—creating action lists or setting up a specific time to engage in something—doesn't have to be complex or difficult. When you focus on a project, goal, or challenging situation that needs immediate attention, you can determine what has to be done first and the order of steps required to take you from A to Z.

> "Do the hard jobs first. The easy jobs will take care of themselves."
>
> — Dale Carnegie

The key to succeeding is knowing the next steps at any given time, the tasks required to complete the work, and subsequently putting together a task list of actions necessary to take you through to the final stages of completion. To get started, ask yourself the following questions:

- What do I have to do next?
- Where do I go from here to get to there?
- What could I be doing to make a significant impact on my personal productivity and efficiency?
- What could I do right now today that would serve to deliver the biggest impact while significantly increasing the quality of life?

For many people, the greatest challenge lies in allocating the right amount of time to doing things in order of importance. It becomes necessary to schedule everything around your priorities, with your purpose as a constant point of reference. You can discipline yourself to make the time for these priorities, while keeping minor tasks on the outside, if only for a short while.

This isn't to say that the little stuff isn't important, but what matters is that it doesn't take precedence over the things that have the highest potential to deliver a positive impact on your way of life. It is essential to keep the big picture at the front at all times. This way, you will follow a logical series of steps to create a desired outcome.

To be truly effective in the areas of your life that matter most, determine the order of your tasks and then allocate time for carrying them out. This method can be used and applied to any situation: planning a trip, developing a new product, building a business, constructing a house, or taking courses at school. Whatever you're focused on, the quality of the results will be in alignment with the organization of the integrated actions and the amount of effort exerted.

The key to accomplishing your dreams and objectives and getting from one point to another is to adopt a systematic approach for conducting your daily, weekly, and monthly tasks. However, it does not end there.

Priority planning entails effectively organizing your schedule around critical matters that make a difference. When you plan effectively, you are operating from a position of power where you don't get sucked into the vortex of everyone else's crises.

Distractions and Priority Choices

When we put the little stuff ahead of the things that matter most, there is a tendency to drift off course and lose focus as concentration falters. When this happens, precious time is wasted. The little things that matter the least often take precedence over what matters the most.

Know what you have to accomplish each day. Stay true to your vision and take the actions required to accomplish your dreams in as little time as possible. With the wave of endless distractions in the world today, which makes unnecessary demands on your valuable (and limited) time, it is easy to lose sight of important things.

Priority planning puts you in a powerful position to accomplish your most critical tasks first, without being pulled into doing things that lead to poor results or unproductive habits. If you don't plan for a successful outcome, you will end up working for someone else's plan.

Remember you have the power to make a choice. You can decide what needs to be done and determine when it can be done. Find the time and place that works best for you. When the big stuff is handled, you can always deal with the countless small stuff that needs to be completed.

Stephen Covey said, "The things that matter most should never be at the mercy of those things that matter least." Although less critical things have their own place, they can often wait. You can prioritize those actions based on all the details that come your way. You can choose to act or react.

Remember that you can't do everything. You can, however, do what matters the most first by making priority choices. Leave the rest for another day.

What is Distracting You?

Right now, make a list of the people, things, or activities that distract you. Is someone constantly calling you to help them out of a crisis? Is it junk email? Do you spend too much time surfing the Internet for useless information? Do you just turn on the TV as a means to kill time?

By digging deep and exposing the areas in which you waste time, you will be able to empower yourself to control impulses that rob you of energy. Everyone has at least one mode of escape. It is something that pulls you off course. By exposing this internal or external weakness, you take away its power. This is a critical step to gaining more time for doing the things that matter.

Now, make a list of things that are consistently distracting you. Then, for everything on your list, write down an alternative action you can do in place of the distraction. For example, if you are distracted by incoming emails, you could simply turn off the auto-alert. You don't have to respond or even look at every single email right away, do you?

Remember that a distraction is nothing more than a bad habit at most times, and habits can be changed with practice and persistence. The key is to make yourself aware of what you are doing at all times. Formulate a new trigger. When you feel the urge to do something that you know is going to cost you time, money, or energy, create a diversion for yourself.

If you are in the habit of wasting time watching TV instead of reading, set out the books you want to read so they are visible. Give yourself twenty-minute time intervals. Discipline yourself and take the high road. You will discover after weeks of persistent practice that the high road is the only road you desire to travel on.

The Crisis Manager and Identifying Your Priority Fields

"I do not equate productivity to happiness. For most people, happiness in life is a massive amount of achievement plus a massive amount of appreciation. And you need both of those things."

— Tim Ferriss

Most people fail to define their priorities because there always seems to be something that demands their attention on the spot: A ringing phone, an unanswered email, or someone with an "urgent" problem.

Finally, at the end of the day, when you actually want to sit down and work, you feel that there is very little mental energy remaining. You have just spent the last twelve hours being busy, and the things you really wanted to do have been left on the back burner.

This is the crisis trap you fall into when the world demands your attention. The workplace, family, friends, society, and more, has caused your habit for setting priorities to diminish. In other words, whatever is in front of you at that moment is served first.

While you are trying to put out a fire in one area, another is starting somewhere else. This eventually results in the formation of a "do it now" habit that keeps you busy. Instead of leading to any long-lasting achievement, the focus is on short-term results.

Let's look at priority areas of your life to apply your full concentration, so you can achieve maximum results and success.

Goal Management: Do you know what your goals are for this week, month, and year? What about today's priority action plan? You can refer to the goal portfolio you created in chapter three.

If you haven't done this yet, do it right now. It only takes a couple of hours to put all your goals and actions on paper, organize them, and then determine which actions to take first. The time you invest in creating a goal portfolio pays back huge returns in the months and years to come.

Relationship Development: Are you spending adequate time building your relationships with friends, family, and coworkers? What about your relationship with yourself? The time you spend with people is an investment, both in their lives and in yours.

It contributes to the quality of friendships, both personal and professional, that you will have for a lifetime. Developing relationships should be one of the highest priorities on your list.

Personal Development: Are you taking care of your personal needs or spending more time fulfilling the needs of others? Are you learning anything new that could help you develop into a stronger, more effective, and happier person? I am not implying that you should disregard others' needs. On the contrary, be as open to helping others as you can be. Just don't forget yourself in the process.

Life Planning: Creating a mission statement, building and maintaining a financial portfolio, or having a dream for the future and working toward that dream is all part of the life planning cycle. Do you have goals for your life? Have you created a mission statement? Do you have a financial target for the next five to ten years and a plan for achieving this target?

Are you allocating enough time each week toward the activities you are passionate about mastering? Do you review these goals each month, and take the time to organize your actions at the beginning of each week? Spend at least two hours per week reviewing your life's plans and goals and your progress.

Having Fun: Yes, having fun and enjoying yourself is a priority, too. Bestselling author of The Road Less Travelled, Dr. M. Scott Peck said, "We must schedule time for fun. It doesn't have to be the last thing you do at the end of a busy workweek. Go to a movie, read a book, or take your children to the park. Enjoy yourself and you will be fulfilling one of the most important priorities for health: having fun!"

The Little Stuff Around the House: Take some time to make getting organized a priority habit. Start with your home. Are there areas that need cleaning? Could you take some old clothes to the second-hand shop? Is there anything that needs to be fixed? Doing these things eliminates procrastination and you will feel better when you've taken care of things.

Is there anything you have a burning desire to do but have been putting on the back burner? This could be a priority issue that you have chosen to avoid. Several years ago, as I was cleaning the house, I found the partial remains of an unfinished book (the one you are holding in your hands right now) and I immediately created a priority action list and went to work on getting it done.

I broke the stages of the work down into micro-steps and set to work on each individual step, giving it my full concentration no matter how small or trivial it seemed. I made a checklist of the steps and ticked each off as they were completed. You can follow the same process for anything you want to get done.

Take a walk around your home to see what is unfinished and make a list. You never know what's lurking under your bed or inside the closet. Once you have a list of projects, choose one, make a list of actions if it is something that can't be done right away, and set out to finish it.

Uncompleted Tasks and Projects

According to personal productivity guru David Allen, you have to regularly write everything that's occupying your mind down on paper and subsequently organize a system for evaluating the actions required for handling everything. There may be dozens of unfinished tasks and numerous projects that have been on the back burner for years. You might be aware of them on a subconscious level, but you must specifically identify with these projects.

Now, make a list of all the things you have been meaning to do but haven't. You can categorize (projects, business, or chores around the house) all the items in this list and decide the action required for completing each of them. You can start right now by taking a look around. Note anything that looks disorganized or out of place.

Is there something you need to do, but you just haven't gotten around to it? If so, write it down.

This is a vital action step to gaining control of your life. Without performing this exercise, you could spend countless weeks or even years struggling to keep up with everything that is demanding your attention. By making a list of all the unfinished business around your desk, on your shelves, in your closets, under the bed, and in your head, you will feel a great sense of relief.

"Much of the stress that people feel doesn't come from having too much to do. It comes from not finishing what they've started."

— David Allen

Above all else, you will be able to sort through everything when you are more aware of what you have. As you become aware of your priorities, the stress of having to take care of everything melts away. Remember that you can't do everything, but you can take care of the things that matter most.

As you work down your list of tasks, you will start to feel a great sense of accomplishment. The more tasks you concentrate on finishing, the more your confidence expands. You can make anything happen as soon as you get organized.

Here are the steps in summary:

1. Make a list of tasks, projects, chores and all work that remains unfinished. Create a list of everything, no matter how small it may seem.

2. Prioritize the items on your list in the order they should be tackled. In this case, it doesn't necessarily mean that you have to do the biggest project on your list first. You might want to start with something small and work your way through before taking on a larger task. The purpose of this is to get something done!

3. For work that requires multiple steps to complete, create a list of tasks that need to be checked off in order to finish the project. Put these mini-tasks in order of importance.

4. Review your progress once a week. Make note of what has been done. Be sure to recognize the progress you're making. Then, take note of what needs to be done this week, next month, and possibly over the next year.

Continue to review your progress and set yourself up with a schedule so you can concentrate on the goal or project at hand.

Action Plan

1. Draw a box on a piece of paper and write down the activities, people, or situations that are really important to you. These are your priority areas. It can include a new project, a family event, or something you just love doing and would like to spend more time on. Write as many things as you want in this box.

2. Make another box on a separate page and write down any distractions that waste your time. Is it TV, too many video games, pleasure-focused activities, or a boss who has you staying late at work every night? Everyone has to face these things, and as soon as you focus on them, you begin losing precious personal time.

3. What is your master goal for this month? Write it down and make a list of priority actions that will enable you to complete this goal. Write down all the actions you can think of, including making phone calls or taking a course at a college. Put these action steps into an organized plan and get to work! It could be anything—an unfinished novel, or even a half-renovated kitchen.

Using the steps outlined in this chapter, make a list of everything you have to accomplish to see this project through to the end. Now, make your list of actions and continue the task.

The Wall of Obstacles

"History has demonstrated that the most notable winners usually encountered heartbreaking obstacles before they triumphed. They won because they refused to become discouraged by their defeats."

— B. C. Forbes

Obstacles are barriers that stand between you and the fulfillment of your dreams. To get from where you are today to the place you desire to be in the not-too-distant future, you will have to face life's challenging roadblocks along the way.

Most of these obstacles can be overcome with a few simple strategies. More difficult challenges require an advanced approach. This could be a shift in personal values, the adoption of new beliefs, or developing a deeper level of wisdom and mindfulness.

In some cases, therapy is required to overcome issues that may be blocking you from reaching your goals.

If you are serious about achieving your dreams and are willing to go to any lengths, you will endure difficulties in which courage and confidence is challenged, beliefs are questioned, and unresolved trauma is confronted. In this place of fear and uncertainty, you will have to face the most terrifying obstacle of all: yourself.

You must prepare yourself to dig in and push through the problems blocking your direct path to freedom. Only by facing obstacles will you be able to make progress. Unfortunately, many people falter as soon as they hit the first wall and realize there's no instant solution that can solve their problems.

An obstacle is blocking your path and appears insurmountable. Unless you can find a way to get past this hurdle, you will always be stuck by challenges that appear larger than you. When you find yourself at this crossroad, remember there is no problem or difficulty too complex that cannot be resolved.

Your success in any situation is measured by your performance in working through problems. If there is a way to avoid dealing with the problem, your first instinct may be to disregard it, bury it, or try to pass it on to someone else.

Either way, you will only seek to defeat yourself. That which you do not confront is unresolved. Even if it is resolved by someone else, this won't help you grow. You must take care of your own weeds in the garden. They are still your weeds—even if someone else pulls them out.

When you pass the buck to someone else, instead of making a real effort to solve the situation, you end up disempowering yourself. You are doing the other person a favor by giving them the opportunity to solve what you passed on. There's nothing wrong with asking for help but be intentional in conquering your own issues.

Life's obstacles present an opportunity to strengthen yourself and become more confident as you defeat your own limitations. One of the greatest measures of successful people is their ability to transcend life's difficulties and overcome the roadblocks that threaten to hold them back. Successful people stand up to challenges that threaten their goals and dreams.

External and Internal Obstacles

"Unless you try to do something beyond what you have already mastered, you will never grow."

— Ronald E. Osborn

I have divided obstacles into two categories: external and internal. We largely create circumstances in our lives through our emotion, thought, action, interaction with people, and the quality of our relationships.

The problems we create because of our direct influence are called internal obstacles. The other set of obstacles is external, and in most cases, has nothing to do with us directly. However, we may be connected to such obstacles, not by choice but by duty or responsibility to seek solutions.

External Obstacles

External obstacles are the unpredictable events thrown in your path when you least expect them. They are created by the situations, circumstances, and natural events that are beyond your control. Whether it is a global crisis that starts on the opposite side of the world or an ill family member who needs your immediate attention, external obstacles challenge your ability to deal with a situation that is not entirely of your own making.

There is very little you can do to prevent these things from happening. However, you can do everything in your control to make the circumstances more favorable. This could mean reaching out to someone who really needs your help. Or, being pulled into a situation either at work or at home where a problem exists and you are expected to provide a successful outcome for other parties.

You may not have created a particular problem, but you could still be a part of the solution.

When a situation that you didn't create arises, instead of responding with fear or by deciding it's "not my problem," condition yourself to adopt a different approach. Consider this a valuable opportunity to step up and take charge. If you feel afraid of the problem, let yourself feel that fear. Take action in the face of what frightens you. Your fearful emotions do not have to control your actions. You can control your emotions by doing something.

You can respond to any situation. If you choose to disregard a certain problem, it will continue to exist. The best time to determine how to deal with an obstacle is when it stands between you and all your hopes and dreams. You may face a situation in which you're asked to find a solution to a problem, and others could be looking to you for guidance.

Regardless of whether the problem is a situation in your company, at home, or in a personal relationship, always ask yourself the following:

What can I do in this situation?
How can I make a difference here?
What actions could I take right now that everyone else is avoiding?

These questions create a higher level of personal empowerment as you start to think about possible solutions.

When you seek solutions to obstacles keeping you stuck, you empower yourself. When you rely on someone else to figure out the answers, you empower them. If you work together to overcome a barrier, you empower each other.

You can develop new methods and solutions for tackling these barriers when they appear and pose as obstacles in your path.

External obstacles include things such as the decisions of others and how they impact you, global economic crisis, war, natural disasters and illness.

You can decide how to handle the situation. Will you let it influence you in a negative manner, draining your energy day after day as the circumstances of the world shape your future? Instead, will you take action to seek out a solution to make the best of the situation at hand?

You always have a choice, in any situation, to do something. Take the lead when you have to and step back to let others deal with the crisis when that's the best thing to do. As long as you are aware of the difference, you can decide either way.

Internal Obstacles

Internal obstacles are problems or conditions that are created through your direct involvement. It may be a situation arising from an unresolved issue, a difficult relationship, or a crisis related to work.

These obstacles can be very threatening because of the personal emotional ties we have to them. With external obstacles, it is much easier when you can acknowledge that you had nothing to do with creating this situation. But personal obstacles are more emotional and tied closely to your feelings of rejection and failure.

We all face countless internal obstacles. Many of these obstacles are small and harmless, so they go unnoticed. Other obstacles, however, may take over our lives. If they are not controlled or removed, their manifestation could make you miserable. These self-defeating behaviors grow from within and threaten to destroy you. They harm you spiritually and negatively influence your confidence and your ability to take a proactive stance.

If they aren't confronted, they act like slow poison. When this happens, we become powerless, foolish, and fatigued. In our efforts to avoid pain and suffering caused by obstacles created by our self-defeating behaviors, we may turn to other methods of escapism (drugs, alcohol, excessive shopping) to relieve our suffering inflicted by this internal enemy. Internal obstacles include things like addictions, grief, trauma, negative thinking and more.

Obstacles that are hidden from view are the most difficult to overcome. Our greatest enemy is within us and remains elusive until strong intervention measures are taken.

Once you have confronted your greatest fears, you will have taken the first step to victory. The stranglehold that these problems have on your life will be defeated and the pathway to a new way of living will appear before you. This is your pathway to freedom. When you face your greatest trial with courage and faith, you are free to walk this path.

Facing your fears and personal demons gives you great strength. When you refuse to be defeated, the chains that bind you are released.

Whether you have an addiction, or you habitually think negatively, the power to change these behaviors lies within you. In the end, you are only as weak as you believe yourself to be.

Obstacles Have a Five-Fold Purpose

"Happiness is dependent on self-discipline. We are the biggest obstacles to our own happiness. It is much easier to do battle with society and with others than to fight our own nature."

— Dennis Prager

An obstacle is not a roadblock; it is a necessary element that serves a purpose. Obstacles help us grow. We tend to think problems will prevent us from moving ahead. Instead, it is by developing solutions to overcome challenges that the greatest growth is achieved.

Here are five reasons why obstacles matter and why we should embrace them as tools that can help us evolve.

1. Obstacles contribute to growth and development.

Develop the attitude that every challenging situation carries an opportunity for you to become stronger. Create a deeper awareness of why this particular problem has come into your life.

It is important to acknowledge that obstacles exist to enable us to evolve and make progress. This builds character, boosts courage, and gives you a deeper feeling of satisfaction once you have effectively worked through a difficult period.

2. Obstacles serve to increase self-confidence and boost self-esteem.

We feel a sense of deep fulfillment by overcoming challenges. This increases confidence and strengthens the belief that nothing is impossible. Instead of being powerless, you become empowered. You develop a strong character.

With every victory, your confidence moves up a notch, making you less fearful of the future. Remember that most people fail because they don't believe in themselves, not because they lack ability.

3. Meeting new challenges expands opportunities.

You can become the master of problem-solving only by facing adversity and the things in life that oppose your ideals or chosen path. Your greatest challenge is to deal with difficult people or unpleasant situations.

These challenges give you an opportunity to become something today that you weren't yesterday, to face problems and find solutions. Your greatest victory lies in facing your deepest fears.

4. Overcoming obstacles puts us in line with our life's purpose.

Dealing with obstacles aligns us with things that are important in our lives. What appears to be a roadblock is actually a tool for enhancing focus and bringing us back to the path that leads to fulfillment. Meet challenges head on, find solutions, and when you can't find the answers you're looking for right away, take the time to explore other possible solutions.

Weigh your decisions carefully. Brainstorm options. Meditate and focus on whatever has led you to this place. Perceive every challenge as a stepping stone to a new level of awareness that draws you closer to your purpose, enabling you to stay on track.

Once you have managed to effectively remove a roadblock, it becomes a part of your life. You don't just throw it away and forget about it. Instead, forge a relationship with each victory. The obstacles in your life have a purpose and, once you have faced them and effectively handled the situation, your life's purpose become clearer.

5. Obstacles serve as your greatest teachers.

Obstacles are not necessarily hindrances designed to cause failure. However, your perception of a significant problem or misfortune in many cases is disillusioned. The obstacle that stands in your way serves as your greatest teacher. You learn the deepest lessons in life by facing the situations that challenge you and by overcoming these opposing forces. Remember that the tougher the challenge, the greater the reward and more valuable the lesson.

Facing the Thirty-Foot Wall

When faced with a situation that we don't know how to deal with, the initial instinct is to react with negative resistance. We approach the solution from an angle of powerlessness. You may say things like, "Well, it's not my problem! I had nothing to do with this!" or catch yourself complaining about the situation and coming up with reasons why it happened, how it could have been avoided, and who is to blame.

Complaining is always a complete waste of resources. It only adds to the problem and offers nothing in exchange.

Complaining about something or someone only makes the situation more unbearable for both the complainer and the people listening to them. You may think that you are getting something off your chest or releasing your frustration surrounding a particular incident, but if you carefully observe how you feel afterward, you'll probably realize that you feel even more stressed and angry. Nothing will have been resolved. Only negative emotions would have been unleashed.

Many of the ways that we deal with problems are based on our experiences, traumas, and old ways that support our limiting beliefs. When we don't know what to do, we react based on old methods that no longer work. We tend to fall into our old patterns, especially when it comes to problem solving, as a means of dealing with our own fears and insecurities. We resist the problem until it becomes someone else's problem or is buried under all the lies we tell ourselves.

One of the first things we tend to do is label the problem with a negative attitude. If it is a person, we come up with damaging labels for them. Labeling something attaches the blame to a person or situation. However, labeling not only disempowers the person being labeled, it also disempowers you.

If a difficult situation arises, avoid the labeling game. For many people, their first reaction is to strap a label on the problem and walk away. They distance themselves from the obstacle as if to say, "There, I just took care of it. Next?"

When faced with a challenge, focus on controlling your initial reactions to the problem. Instead of picking up the phone and launching a complaint session, think of effective solutions you could try to make the situation better. Instead of reacting negatively and saying there is no solution, first identify exactly what the difficulty is, and then mind map the solutions to reach a conclusion.

Try to find solutions to everything. Take time to think things through. Brainstorm ideas and talk with people positively instead of labeling or gossiping. This is "obstacle avoidance," and it is the most unproductive approach you can take.

Perceive every problem as an opportunity to expand your growth. Listen to what your emotions are telling you and not your mind. The mind is full of ego and rarely works to resolve anything when left to its own devices. When you follow your heart in any situation, everything will be the better for it.

The Formula: A Four-Step Process

"Concern yourself more with accepting responsibility than with assigning blame. Let the possibilities inspire you more than the obstacles discourage you."

— Ralph Marston

There is an effective formula or process that can be applied to almost any challenging situation or difficulty you are facing. When confronted with a problem that seems too big to conquer, you can find a way to overcome it by using the four-step process below.

1. Identify the obstacle.

Describe the obstacle in one sentence. Do you want to buy a house but you don't have enough money? Do you have to speak with your boss about a problem with your work? Is your son or daughter experiencing a problem at school and they need your help? Are you working on a project that is over budget and behind schedule?

No matter what the situation is, the first step to working toward a solution is to identify it. Write it out on paper to make it real. Don't keep anything in your head and try to work it out. That's the worst place for a challenge to exist. Then, once you have identified the problem with absolute clarity....

2. Mind map potential solutions.

Now that you have clearly defined the obstacle, it is easier to draw ideas on what actions to take. For the second step, create a "branch of ideas," or a mind map of possible solutions. By putting your ideas to paper, you can see with greater clarity the solution to overcoming your obstacles. People get stuck when they hold those ideas in their head. The mind has a way of latching onto a problem and making it bigger by focusing on the problem instead of the way out.

You can now write in point form as many possible solutions as you can think of.

3. Select the best choice.

Next, from the list of options, choose the best one. Write down the best solution and work toward taking immediate action. It may be that the obstacle requires several solutions.

In this case, you can prioritize the options in the order of importance. Take action on the first choice and once complete, move to the next possible solution on your list. Keep working through it until you have successfully overcome the problem.

4. Follow up on the outcome.

After applying the formula to your situation, you may not have an immediate outcome. The application of your solutions may take time to work. The final stage is to follow up on the results.

Did you get the outcome you wanted? Did you experience a different result than what you expected? If you didn't get what you were hoping for, continue to apply other solutions. Just because something didn't deliver the first time doesn't mean the situation is hopeless. For every obstacle you face, there is a way to overcome it.

Action Plan

1. What obstacles are holding you back right now? Do you have a plan for getting past them? Apply the above formula to help you develop solutions.
2. Everyone has at least one self-defeating behavior that challenges them. Write down your self-defeating behavior and the steps you plan to take to overcome this behavior.
3. Create a mind map of solutions for this scenario and put your ideas into action.
4. Next, write down an internal obstacle you're currently facing. Subsequently, think about this obstacle and brainstorm solutions.

5. Write about an external obstacle you had to face. Were you successful in dealing with it? If so, how did you do it? If not, what would you have done differently?

Getting Over the Past

"Don't dwell on what went wrong. Instead, focus on what to do next. Spend your energies on moving forward toward finding the answer."

— Denis Waitley

The past is a fingerprint of the life that once was, now stamped permanently in the roots of your mind as memories. Lingering in the shadows of our past days, it serves as a reminder of whom we were, what we have done, and all of life's experiences collaged together that have brought us to the present moment.

Your present is the result of all your past choices and decisions. You have built the path you are on. Having accepted this, you are responsible for where you are today.

Everyone's past tells a different story. Some people have had it good while living a life of comfort. Others have had a life of struggle and hardship and suffered more than others. Nobody's past is a perfect fairy tale. It is the experiences you have lived through and events that took place that tells the story of your life, both light and dark.

The past holds the deepest secrets of the soul and unveils the truth that serves as a reminder of the lessons you must never forget.

If you spend endless hours obsessing about the past, you will be lost in the present moment. You neglect the present moment when you choose to live in past memories. You end up losing golden opportunities if you are in the habit of obsessing about yesterday.

Living in the past with the hope of changing it, or wishing it'd been different somehow, puts a cripple on the future. You can't have both worlds. You need to choose one. As long as you are hanging out with the ghosts of the past, you will never move on. If you are locked into an abysmal state of nostalgic fantasy, you cannot focus on the only period of your life that really matters: the present.

The unconscious habit of redialing past events is like picking up the phone, dialing a number that has been out of service for twenty years, and expecting someone to answer. The simple truth is that the script cannot be rewritten. You are here and that's all that matters.

The haunts of the past are with you and may always be, but they don't have to control your future. You can control the tendency to relive the past by awakening to the notion that you have choices in every moment of every day, and how you choose to live each day is up to you.

Resentment: The Suffering Path

"Resentment is like a glass of poison that a man drinks; then he sits down and waits for his enemy to die."

— Nelson Mandela

One of the greatest causes of misery is failing to resolve resentments linked to past events. Holding on to anger and bitter feelings of the past instigates a cycle of negative emotional trauma. Resentment is a form of negative energy that eats away at us over time, leading to depression, anxiety, and other negative emotions.

These resentments are the judgments and perceptions formed about other people, places, or events that have wronged, harmed, or victimized us, as perceived by the ego-mind. Just because you are angry about something, doesn't necessarily mean you are right about it.

You might have a good reason for your bitterness: a case of dishonesty, theft, abuse, or something said or done that caused you some form of emotional, physical, or mental harm. You have latched onto this pain and are refusing to give in or let go. Years later, the anger and bitterness has turned against you, transforming it into your worst enemy.

Taking on resentment is like swallowing a bitter pill. You are linking the pain and suffering of the past to the thoughts and emotions of the present. Bitter, deep-seated anger and resentment builds over the years.

Some people hold onto deep grudges, as if it brings some kind of relief to remember what was done to them by someone who betrayed their trust.

This is the ego's defense for dealing with wrongdoings. The ego wants revenge. It wants the other party to suffer, and it will not rest until justice is served. Until that day comes, it will remain in a state of bitter anger, seeking ways to win.

A Waste of Life

Resentment festers in the conscious mind and creates a negative state so powerful that not a single day goes by without feeling bitter over old wounds. Carrying around resentment leads to unhappiness and a sad waste of life.

Resentment robs you of the present by focusing on the past. You hold onto your pain by refusing to let it go, as if you have the right to be angry. The wounds never have a chance to heal. In fact, over time, this pain can cause severe mental trauma and illness.

Resentment blocks all positive thoughts from creating new experiences. You can't build the future if you are trying to reconstruct past events. You will never move on if you are too busy hating someone for something they did years ago. If you're harboring resentment right now, ask yourself if it has made your life any better. Would you really feel better if you could exact some kind of retribution?

When you resent someone or something, you are invariably handing over your power to that person or situation. A mentor once said to me, "The definition of suffering is being bitter toward someone and having him or her be completely unaware of it."

While you are busy wasting your creative thoughts and energy on people you don't like for whatever reason, they are living their lives elsewhere, completely oblivious to your anger.

Do yourself a favor and find a way to get over the pain caused by past events. I am not suggesting that you try to forget these painful events, but how you choose to deal with them is entirely up to you. The grief you're holding onto is your responsibility. It is time to let go, move on, and live your life.

There is a Solution

A suggestion that was once made by a good friend of mine changed my perspective regarding situations about which I was bitter. This person, who was much wiser and full of spiritual energy, advised me to pray for the people and things that made me angry. He said, "To hold onto the things that make you miserable is the worst form of suffering. By identifying your resentments, you free yourself from the emotional suffering they are causing."

So, taking this advice, I set out to free myself from the resentments holding my mind prisoner.

I had to get to the core of these negative feelings if I wanted to find peace. I had to get honest with myself and do a deep analysis of my fears.

I was asked to make a list of resentments as a way to cleanse my heart and mind from pain.

Here are the steps for working through resentment:

Take an Inventory of Your Resentment

I created a "resentment inventory" and included the names of the people and events I resented as well as the reason behind my resentment. Here are six steps to help you prepare your resentment inventory.

- Create a list. Make a list of all the people, places, events, and/or principles that you resent. Write down the names of all the people and places and details of the events.

- List the causes. Now, go back to the top of the list and in another column or on a separate piece of paper, write down the cause of the resentment for each item. Why are you angry? What happened?

- How has this resentment affected you? Next, write down how each event affected you. Did it impact your wealth, self-esteem, emotional state, or security?

- What is the benefit of holding on? Most people feel they are gaining something by resenting the source of their pain. Write down what you are gaining from continuing to hold onto your resentment.

- What is your role in this situation? As someone who has been wronged, you might think you are the victim and therefore take no responsibility. However, what thoughts are you harboring that feed into this? How do you continue to hand over your personal power to the source of your resentment?

- How are you contributing to the situation? The people or institutions that you dislike, regardless of the reasons, are not going to change. This leaves you with only one choice: you must change your perceptions and attitude. Let others change theirs. You have the personal power to evolve beyond your present condition. Now, write down exactly how you are feeding into this insanity. Once you identify the pattern, you can work on a solution for stopping the cycle.

- Take inventory regularly. Do an inventory of your resentments every three to six months. Check for new resentments that may have cropped up and use these steps for dealing with them.

Regret: Obsession to Change the Past

"The power for creating a better future is contained in the present moment: You create a good future by creating a good present."

— Eckhart Tolle

Regret is an obsession. Although it's normal to feel remorse or disappointment because something was or wasn't done, or a situation didn't work out exactly the way that you planned, regretting past events can reinforce feelings of failure and remorse.

Regret is a form of emotional suffering. It focuses on past events that occurred with an outcome that is perceived to be negative. Your expectations were not met and you are now left feeling cheated or disappointed.

Another form of regret is for things you didn't do when you had the opportunity, resulting in a feeling of deep loss. If you faced such an event, the suffering may persist and in some severe cases, the pain lasts a lifetime.

Regret that is not dealt with or accepted eats away at you over time. You end up feeling as if you are constantly living with the ghosts of your past, forever haunted by memories of events that can never be changed. When you hold onto regrets, you are living in an illusion and clinging to false hopes.

Identifying things in your life for which you are grateful is an effective way to deal with regret. There may have been a different outcome had you done things differently, but how do you know it would have been better?

The choices and decisions you make at any given moment are based on who you are at that time. You did what you felt was right. You will do what you feel needs to be done today based on who you are right now and the information you possess to make those choices.

If you do have regrets—a job you lost, a relationship that didn't work out, or a decision you made that ended badly—would your life be different if everything had worked out according to plan? Is everything in life supposed to work out perfectly?

I was once told that regret, although very real, is an illusion of the worst kind. It is a false belief that convinces you that all your choices and past experiences have failed you. This simply isn't true. You had certain expectations that were never met, and when the outcome you desperately wanted failed to come true, you feel regretful.

Life is a process, a series of wins and losses, triumphs and failures. None of it's all good or bad, but our thinking makes it so.

Living in the Present Moment

The past is inescapable. The events that took place either yesterday or twenty years ago, are now unchangeable and a part of your history. The mind forges a powerful anchor with the past. This is the beginning of a state of disillusion.

You may have heard that some people live in the past. Well, this refers to those who exist in neither the past nor the present. They can no longer separate what has happened and what is taking place in the present moment. The truth is that our mind can only exist in one place at any given time.

If you are obsessing about something that happened in the morning or ten days ago, you are not in the present moment and are therefore lost in the illusion. The only way to be real and deal with ghosts of the past is to be present, right here and now, in this moment.

To exist in the present moment brings you peace of mind and relaxes the senses. If you dwell on past events by reliving those moments, you lose precious time that could be spent building new experiences today and tomorrow.

The experiences of yesterday cannot be rebuilt. What happened in the past cannot be undone. Let those towers of memories exist as they are. Focus on your gratitude for what you have in the moment. Everything else is just an illusory state of existence.

The Past Is an Illusion

Once an event is over and has moved into the past, it enters into a state of illusion. It no longer exists in the present moment. It is human nature to habitually obsess about past events. The illusion becomes our past, present, and future reality.

The longer we fixate on past events, the more the past becomes the present, and the present becomes the future. People who are trapped in a spin cycle of trying to create the future based on past experiences only end up recreating the same results they experienced before. Nothing new is created. The past becomes the future once again.

> "We are products of our past, but we don't have to be prisoners of it."
>
> — Rick Warren

There is nothing wrong with telling tales of the past or thinking about past events. Everyone has a past. Everyone has a story to tell that is unique to that person, and they are shaped and molded by their past.

When your present mind exists in the past, it becomes lost in mirrors of disillusionment. Instead of creating a better future, you recreate the history of past events without a future. When this happens, the past is never finished so long as it is kept alive by the reminder of past regrets and failures.

Think of the past as much as you need to and use it to your advantage as a measuring stick to remind yourself of how far you have come and how much you have grown. If it's used as a form of punishment, the pain of self-loathing can turn into a destructive force.

Free yourself by living in the present. This will help you break the habit and lose the mental attraction to return to past memories.

Forgiveness: The Path to Peace

Forgiveness is the path that leads to a peaceful existence, not only for you but for others as well. It is the solution to moving beyond the suffering inflicted by resentment and regret.

Forgiveness eliminates pain and guilt, isolation and anger. It replaces these emotions with acceptance and silences the mind. When you forgive someone else for a perceived wrongdoing or for hurting you, a sliver of light opens up in your consciousness, enabling you to introduce change.

If you take this quantum leap and practice forgiving yourself, you will move into a higher state of consciousness. This will place you in a position of personal empowerment and create a new passage for positive events of the future. Although resentment and regret holds you back, forgiveness propels you forward. It cures all ills of fear, doubt, and confusion.

By relinquishing your connection with the past deeds and outcomes that cannot be altered, you seek to create new opportunities and increase your chances of achieving success. Instead of recreating and reliving the past, you open up higher realms of thought. This expands to creating a greater positive outflow of energy and helps you find fulfillment.

Forgiveness is a positive step toward releasing the pain that you've been holding onto. You don't have to forget what has happened, but by undertaking the courageous act of forgiving someone, you are giving yourself and the other person the permission to move on, to let go, and to heal. Forgiving extricates you from playing the role of a weak victim and empowers you to take the path of the courageous.

Just as you choose to resent someone for the harm and hurt they caused, you can choose to forgive the outcome. It takes a big-hearted person to forgive and to practice forgiveness. People who choose to remain in a state of bitter resentment also remain small in character. Forgiveness is a win-win situation in which everyone benefits.

Action Plan

1. Do you have any deep-seated resentment toward a person, place, or event that happened in your life? How can you release this resentment and anger? Does it make you feel good to harbor this resentment or do you feel a deep sense of suffering? Follow the steps mentioned in this chapter to conduct a regular inventory every few months.

2. Write about a major life event or relationship from the past. How did this change you?

3. How much time and energy do you spend thinking about past events, trauma, and relationships? Do these memories fill you with positive or negative energy? How do you feel about your life in general?

4. Are you deeply satisfied with where you are today? If the answer is no, what are you going to do about it?

5. If you were given the chance to alter any past event or deed, what would it be? Why would you choose to change this event? If this event hadn't occurred, would your life be different today? If so, how would it be different? More importantly, how do you know your life would have turned out better?

Turning Failure into Victory

"There is no failure except in no longer trying. There is no defeat except from within, no really insurmountable barrier save our own inherent weakness of purpose."

— Frank McKinney

Excuses are false justifications created to convince us why we can't live the way we want to. This is a powerful form of self-deception— a lie within a lie that keeps us trapped. Excuses that support our failures are based on a foundation of false beliefs.

Nothing is possible when you are afraid to try new things or explore possibilities. This level of fear seeks to destroy all potential for growth and development.

Created through multiple fears—the fear of failure, the fear of rejection, the fear of success, the fear of living, the fear of change, or the fear of not measuring up to expectations—we allow pathways of negativity to have absolute control over our lives.

If you believe in the reasons you can't, you will never be successful in discovering what you can do when a shift in perspective or attitude takes place.

But there is a way to overcome and defeat this. By talking back with confidence and taking action against voices of self-doubt, excuses lose their power of reasoning. Once you stop creating excuses for why you can't, you develop a new attitude and a new way of thinking.

When you develop the habit of thinking positively and turning every negative situation into a chance to expand and grow, the excuses no longer have any support to control your thoughts or actions. You are free to make positive choices that lead toward successful outcomes instead of failure.

The Iron Will

Failure is a part of living. Regardless of profession, wealth or social status, it happens to everyone. Failing is one of the prime necessities for self-development and growth.

The more chances you take to try different things, the more you increase the risk of failing. The only people I know of who never make mistakes or fail at something are those who never try anything different. They don't accept new challenges or have the desire to be challenged in any way. They stay stuck, not because they can't but by deciding they won't. They follow the same routine every day and take as few risks as possible to avoid stumbling and looking foolish.

If you fall into this category, you might reduce your risk of failing, but you will never break through your own limitations, either. You create a comfort zone that eventually turns into a prison and significantly reduces your chances of achieving the level of success you desire.

Many of our failures have been painful and unforgettable. Relationships that never made it, bad investments, dead-end jobs or embarrassing moments that left you traumatized. It is so painful that our society has conjured up thousands of ways to avoid failing.

The message we have received is clear. Failure is not acceptable. People who fail are punished, held back, ridiculed, or rejected.

We fear looking bad, standing out as someone who never made it, or having to explain ourselves to others when we're criticized for failing.

What is the secret of those who get what they want?

Read this statement and commit it to memory:

People who succeed in spite of failures are made of an iron will that few others possess. They keep trying. When one path doesn't work, they try another. With every failure, they succeed because they are getting closer to achieving their goals.

Whatever we desire is within the realm of possibility, but our negative thinking supports the self-doubt that drives away chances of success. Negative thoughts create beliefs like, "I can't do it" or "I'm not cut out for that" or "Someone else will come up with a better idea." You have to eliminate this pattern of destructive thinking before it has time to complete its cycle.

The only way to defeat this habit is to replace the negative approach with more positive and effective solutions. Decide that no matter what difficulty you are facing, there is a way to succeed.

No matter the obstacle or challenge, you will face your darkest hour and persevere. It is this iron will that cuts through the fear and removes obstacles—the willingness to do whatever it takes to achieve a vision, to accomplish a magnificent goal, and to do everything you can to overcome self-defeat.

Excuses: Pathways to Failure

"Remember your dreams and fight for them. You must know what you want from life. There is just one thing that makes your dream become impossible: the fear of failure."

— Paulo Coelho

Forming excuses is a method used to avoid the fear of taking a risk. Instead of just going for it, people are too afraid to risk looking stupid, or damaging their egos through embarrassment. We would rather take the easy way out and make excuses.

The justifications created that force you to submit to passive inactivity are more damaging than the worst of all failures you could endure. The definition of a true failure isn't someone who tried and never succeeded, but rather someone who never had the courage to try in the first place.

By failing to act, you produce the same results as if you had tried and failed. So, wouldn't it be better to just give it a shot? Would you rather take a chance and see what happens?

Failing to pursue the things you want in life is a failure in disguise. We use excuses to defend ourselves from the hurts of the world as we build walls that protect limited interests and fragile egos, and to preserve the limited field of vision through which we see the world. Your excuses for not pursuing your dreams might appear to be valid, but under the surface is a path that leads to false reasoning and bitter defeat.

Here are some of the excuses we use to convince ourselves that something just isn't a good idea:

"I am too old for that."
"It didn't work for my friends or neighbors, so why should it work for me?"
"The initial investment is just too much. I can't afford to lose that money."

"I've been working at this job for twenty years, so it's too late to change now."

When you make excuses for not taking action, it strengthens your determination to follow the path of least resistance. The ego uses excuses to control your situation, whether you love it or hate it. A day will come when someone else will take the risk that you didn't and they will succeed where you failed.

Their ultimate success will become your tragic failure. Their gain becomes your loss. They might stumble a few times before getting it right, but they will eventually get it, and they will prosper from the success you could have had.

"Fear: False Evidence Appearing Real."

If you want to avoid this, the key is to not think about what you have to lose if you fail, but rather what you have to gain if you succeed. This shift in perception is powerful. One train of thought keeps you stuck in scarcity (I might lose what I have) and the other way of thinking focuses on abundance (I'll gain so much if I succeed).

When it's difficult or seemingly impossible to achieve your goal, make a list of the good things you will gain. Don't give yourself permission to fail. Many people give up just short of the finish line, and they have no idea how close they were. Hang onto your vision until you've succeeded.

Make it a habit to avoid making excuses. Do not accept anything as being impossible to obtain until you've exhausted every known effort to succeed.

Create enough positive reasons as to why you should do it. If you find yourself making up multiple reasons why you can't, step back and analyze how you feel at that moment. In many cases, these negative feelings influence the justifications we create.

You can change your excuses from words of weakness to words of power that inspire and encourage you to overcome your fears.

Talking Back to Your Excuses

The key to facing your personal fears is to take away the power of negative ideas and concepts by removing any unhealthy thoughts that have constructed a false reality. Talk back to your excuses.

These excuses are the same ones you've been using for years to keep the lies real. To avoid facing challenges and grasping opportunity, we create excuses as to why we can't. This behavior of negative self-talk can be diverted with practice, eventually removed, and replaced with more positive, high-powered images of yourself taking on more proactive roles.

Too many people have grown old and realized they could have been more and done more, but fear held them back. Now the fear is a different kind—the fear of knowing they will never have the chance to do the things they always wanted to do.

Regret Before Dying

Bonnie Ware was a nurse who worked in palliative care for many years. Her patients were people who went home to die. Bonnie spent time with each one before they passed away. She asked them to share regrets they had during their life. Common themes emerged from the interviews. This was the core message many had in common:

> I wish I'd had the courage to live a life true to myself, not the life others expected of me.

When you reach the end of your life, will you look back without regret? If you have regrets, what are they? Is it too late to change these events?

The past cannot change, but we can make a difference today. What dreams have you been putting off? Are you still waiting for happiness instead of creating it for yourself?

Regardless of your age, it is never too late to do what you've always wanted to do. Remember you have the power to reinvent who you are at any given time. You can make priority decisions to live in a way that expresses fully who you are as an individual.

The terminal patients interviewed by Bonnie Ware held deep regrets for things they never did and fears that held them back. By failing to make choices that can change your destiny, you are setting yourself up for regret. Instead, choose to become your absolute best.

Your dreams are too important to fall victim to excuses. Start converting excuses into positive words of empowerment. You are not powerless; you wield great power from within.

Viktor Frankl's Message

Viktor Frankl spent three years under the harshest conditions imaginable in the three worst holocaust camps from 1942 to 1945. His story is told in his book, Man's Search for Meaning.

The greatest lesson Viktor spoke of states:

"Everything can be taken from a man but one thing: the last of human freedoms—to choose one's attitude in any given set of circumstances, to choose one's own way."

Regardless of what others do to us, how they act, or the harm they inflict, there is one constant truth: We are in control of our own mind and will.

By giving in and allowing others to control our emotions and thoughts, we are handing them the power to do as they want. We can't always choose our environment or circumstances. But what we can do is choose how we react. Will you say yes, no, or nothing at all?

Will you act the part of a helpless victim or decide that you are stronger than any of life's difficulties?

28 · SCOTT ALLAN

You can only be defeated when you make the choice to do nothing.

You have complete power over your attitude at all times. It is the one thing nobody can take from you. You might lose all your possessions, your home, and your freedom, but you'll always have the right to choose how you respond to the situation.

The Power of Choice

"Some of our important choices have a time line. If we delay a
decision, the opportunity is gone forever. Sometimes our
doubts keep us from making a choice that involves change.
Thus, an opportunity may be missed."

— James E. Faust

What's important is not whether you lose or fail—it's what you do
after you fail that matters. Will you make an excuse to avoid trying
it again? Will you take the easy and safe path, treading lightly without
any risk of stumbling? Or will you embrace your greatest moment
of defeat and turn it into a victory? Are you willing to rise up to meet
the next challenge?

There is a choice to make. Embrace your failures and look for the
chance to turn a loss into a win. We are educated to think that losing
is all about failing and failing is bad. But it's not. When we stumble
and nothing works out the way it should have, it isn't the end of the
world. You can bounce back, get up again and give it another shot.
Most things you are afraid to fail at are really golden opportunities
in disguise. You can choose to ignore these opportunities or take a
chance and act on them.

If you listen to your fear and react to it by not taking action, you will
be paralyzed indefinitely, unable to think or act. Your fears will win
and you will be defeated at every turn. You must be willing to rise
up again after experiencing those continuous knockdowns, and to
refuse to give in when the odds are stacked against you.

A mentor of mine had a saying: "Always be the last man standing."
In a race, after everyone else has given up, you are the one still trying
to reach the finish line. When the market turns bad and you just
suffered a financial hit, you'll be looking for ways to make more
money. When people say that what you are chasing is impossible,
become a believer in the impossible. This is the attitude that
champions adopt.

You can create a motivating positive force by pushing forward, working with your fear and using it as leverage. It's like molding clay. Until you pick it up and start working with it, it remains in its original state. You have the power of choice to create whatever you desire, regardless of present conditions.

Take Charge and Make a Choice

You can start today by taking charge and accepting full responsibility for your life. Live the empowered lifestyle you know you want.

As you learn to talk back to negative messages, you will experience change. Stop convincing yourself why you can't and tell yourself why you can, and the reasons why you feel you deserve this—because you do!

Our excuses are convincing, but they won't stand a chance against the counterattack of a positive statement. For a long time, I used to say to myself, "Why me? Why would anyone want to hire me? Why should someone want to pay me for my work when there's always someone out there who can do it better? Who is going to believe in me when I can't even believe in myself? What do I have to offer?"

I realized these questions were negative and could only lead deeper into thinking like a failure. I took a different approach and started asking, "Hey, why not me?" When you find yourself making a negative excuse, identify the source and replace it with the opposite.

Take a look at the following examples.

I will get to it someday.

Get started on your dream today. If you wait for someday, you will never do it. All your excuses are running out with each new day. It is today that presents the greatest opportunity. Will you seize it, or will you wait for a someday that may never arrive?

I lack the discipline to succeed.

Nobody lacks discipline. We lack worthy goals that motivate and inspire us to take immediate action. If you think you have no discipline, it is because you have goals that don't motivate you or get you excited enough to do anything about it.

Write down your goals as soon as possible and get to work on them. Discipline is not something you are born with. It is a practice you work at to become proficient. Start disciplining your words and thoughts to work for you instead of against you.

I lack the education and knowledge to be successful.

An expensive education from a prestigious university does not guarantee instant success. You still have to work at it. For years I believed that a lack of education or having extensive knowledge was an obstacle for me, until I remembered that Albert Einstein never finished high school, yet he changed the world with his vision, theories, and ideas. It is not a lack of education that causes great failures. It is a lack of imagination.

I was brought up to be ordinary.

It is perfectly acceptable to be ordinary. In a sense, we all are just trying to do our best with what we have. When you come to realize your life's purpose, you have an opportunity to become more than just ordinary. You can do great things, but still do them in an ordinary fashion.

How you were raised only influences outcomes to a point. You make the decision as to whether or not you want to do things the way you were trained to do them.

People who have achieved great things are still ordinary people. They are just ordinary people who accomplished great things because they committed to mastering their craft.

I have no time for my dreams.

If you have no time for dreams, what do you have time for?

It's all been done before.

Great discoveries have been made over the last few decades that have challenged the human imagination in ways never dreamed possible a hundred years ago. It is also true that great ideas are explored every day, and sometimes we lose faith in our ideas or planning because we fear someone else already got there first.

However, it hasn't all been done before or we would be living in a world without any growing needs. The world is still in need of new ideas and visions. Sometimes these ideas build upon what has already been created, and other times a new door is opened leading to future innovative ideas and dynamic pathways.

Develop a Steve Jobs Attitude:
The New Challenge Approach

"For the past 33 years, I have looked in the mirror every morning and asked myself: 'If today were the last day of my life, would I want to do what I am about to do today?' And whenever the answer has been 'No' for too many days in a row, I know I need to change something."

— Steve Jobs

When legendary innovator Steve Jobs approached his engineers with the design for one of his products, he was met with repeated skepticism and told again and again that it couldn't be done. But Jobs had a different approach to everything. He knew that if you could imagine it, it could be done.

Jobs willed his creative imagination into existence because he knew anything he wanted that didn't yet exist could be his if he wanted it enough. Despite the resistance he faced, Steve Jobs became one of the world's greatest innovators. He accepted no excuses, not from himself or from the hundreds of people who worked for him.

I call this the Steve Jobs approach. Anything is possible, and if you put aside the fear and doubt, you will push yourself to the next level. As you rise up, you will bring those who believe in you along for the journey.

It is an amazing thing to conquer one's weaknesses, and better yet, to watch others around you rise up to reach their greatest potential and evolve. Once you decide it's possible, you carve out a new path for yourself.

Applying the New Challenge Approach

Decide right now that you are going to adopt a new challenge approach to every tough obstacle, situation, or problem. Refuse to pass it off on someone else or ignore it. You could be facing a great challenge that will turn into your biggest achievement.

Just as Steve Jobs did, hold yourself to the highest possible standards and do not step down, give in, or give up for any reason. Do not let fear overtake you. Do not live below your potential. Always leap for the next plateau. If you leap with faith, you will make the impossible a reality.

No matter what others might say, if the world's greatest creative visionaries followed through on listening to the rest of the world's doubts, we would still be traveling by horse and buggy and reading books by candlelight. What challenges are you going to take from this day forward? Will you hesitate and give up, or will you fight for what you believe in?

You have the power to choose and be anything you want to be. Dig in. Work hard. Get enthusiastic about living life your way. Seek to inject passion into doing what you love. Take affirmative action where you know you can make a difference. You might fail, but don't allow yourself to be defeated. Keep pushing forward until you have built your dreams from a simple idea into your vision of a new reality.

Once your excuses are removed, you will realize through careful observation that those with no money have the opportunity to make a fortune and become richer than those already in possession of great wealth. Men and women with little training or education can excel and become more in demand than those with years of experience.

People born destitute, handicapped, and with seemingly very few resources can make a larger difference in the world than those who already have riches. In the end, it's not the amount of wealth that makes people rich but having a wealthy attitude.

Try new things and give yourself permission to fail. If you don't succeed at something the first time, try doing it a different way. One of the skills of mastery is discovering the ways that don't work so that you can develop better methods. Every time you get results you don't want, keep shifting your game plan.

Make the necessary adjustments again and again until you get it right. When you find yourself drifting off course, make corrections until you reach your destination. Remember, if Thomas Edison could fail over 10,000 times, you and we can afford to do it at least once.

Action Plan

1. On a sheet of paper, make a list of the excuses you use to avoid living the life you want. How do these excuses benefit you? What do you have to gain by reasoning with your excuses.

2. What are your fears? How can you start to work on overcoming these fears? Write down your top five fears. Now, next to each fear, write down two actions you can take to try to overcome them.

3. On a sheet of paper, put a line down the middle of the page. In the left-hand column, write down ten to fifteen excuses you have used in the past to avoid doing something. In the right-hand column, write down the actions you plan to use to fight back. These are your new weapons against excuses that have been holding you back.

4. What is your biggest failure? How did it make you feel? What did you learn from it? Has it stopped you from taking greater risks? If so, how can you turn this failure into a positive experience?

5. How are you going to apply the new challenge approach to make serious changes in your life? Write down a great idea or a change you want to make, and then apply the new challenge approach to make it happen.

Building a Life Beyond Fear

"You gain strength, courage, and confidence by every experience in which you really stop to look fear in the face. You are able to say to yourself, 'I lived through this horror. I can take the next thing that comes along.'"

— Eleanor Roosevelt

Fear. Why is fear such a powerful force in our lives? Some people face their fears and do incredible things, while others find themselves unable to. Ask yourself why you are afraid. What makes you shrink away from following your dreams?

We are all afraid to a certain degree. We can't remove our fears, we can only work with them and seek the best solutions to removing them. Fear is a part of our lives. If you feel ashamed or embarrassed because you're afraid, it's okay. It doesn't matter. What's important is that you can do something about it.

Will you stay afraid and let it run your life? Sadly, many do this and they end up miserable and filled with uncertainty. They walk around empty and vulnerable, worried about what the future will bring.

When fear dictates how you feel emotionally, and it stops you from doing what you truly desire, you are at the breaking point of decision. It's the moment that changes everything. You can decide right now to empower your life or live disempowered and scared.

We must move beyond fear if we are to succeed. If you're trapped in a fearful lifestyle of procrastination, self-perpetuating lies about who you are, or working a job you hate because you are afraid of failing, you are sealing your fate. You will get older and one day it will be too late. You'll realize all the opportunities you could have had are gone.

Don't let that happen, my friends.

Life beyond fear means thinking and doing even when you are scared. The time is now and not tomorrow. I spent many years talking about the things I'd do tomorrow, but when tomorrow came, I was doing something else. Tomorrow never arrives because it is always one day ahead. You only have today, and what you do with it is up to you.

But just remember that it's not your fear that's in the way. It is your own mind interfering. Your mind is telling you to ignore the risks because you might lose. Don't make any effort because you might fail at it. Don't ask for what you really want because you might get rejected and you'll be humiliated. Don't quit your job and do the work you love because you've had this job forever and you might fail.

Fear can be a powerful motivator. It motivates you to do something about your situation. It can also serve as your worst inhibitor by keeping you scared. The difference is made by how you perceive this fear.

Will you use it to leverage your actions, or will you allow it to hold you back?

Fear is communicated to our subconscious minds. But how do we gain perspective? How do we remove these fears? How can we live an empowered life if we can't gain power over our fears?

Breaking the Barrier of Fear

"Fear keeps us focused on the past or worried about the future.
If we can acknowledge our fear, we can realize that right now
we are okay. Right now, today, we are still alive, and our bodies
are working marvelously. Our eyes can still see the beautiful
sky. Our ears can still hear the voices of our loved ones."

— Thich Nhat Hanh

We know this life can be so much more than it is. We decide the
path we want to take. By making a conscious choice, we can change
everything in an instant. We know our fears are the barriers to
everything we've ever wanted.

Imagine yourself standing on one side of a rapid river, while
everything you've ever wanted is on the other side: people you love,
or things you've always wanted to buy but never could. Maybe you
want to own your own home. What would your life be like if you
could get to the other side? Imagine the possibilities. Visualize
yourself on the other side of that river.

There is risk involved. Very few have crossed this river. Many failed.
You can stay where you are and live a life empty of passion. You
will be unhappy, but at least you'll be safe on your side of the river.
Or you can take a chance and risk it all. Jump in and start swimming.

To get where you want to be, you have to cross the river and risk
getting swept away. You dip your foot in. Sensing the violent waters,
you pull back. Then you think for a long time about whether you
should or shouldn't.

This time, you go in up to your knees and you're pushing your fear
away for a few seconds. You are pushing yourself beyond your
comfort zone. You almost go all the way in, but then you pull back.

Now you have a taste of courage. Five minutes ago, you were
terrified to go near the water. Now you've gone in up to your knees.
What if you pushed further?

How can you get to the other side? To live an empowered life, you have to find a way. If you stay where you are, living within your safety zone and refusing to get your feet wet, don't complain when things fail to go the way you expected. By not taking action, you are making a choice.

It is a choice to accept your current situation as it is. It is a choice to stay where you are, feeling unfulfilled and restless. Meanwhile, your heart has a deeper longing to be on the other side of the river.

We can break this down to a simple choice. You can take the steps necessary by jumping into the river and swimming as hard and fast as you can. This doesn't mean you will make it. You could get swept downstream and fail. But you can always try again and again.

The fear of what might happen if you fail is keeping you stuck. You can take action in two ways. You can jump in and give it all you've got. This works for a lot of people because it allows them to commit completely.

You can also take small steps, test the water, and emerge from your safety zone gradually. Then, when you're ready, leap. If massive action is not your style, take small steps and start building momentum.

The man who jumps into the river knows that he can barely swim, but the risk of staying put is equally terrifying. He makes it to the halfway mark and then he gets into trouble. The water is stronger than he anticipated. He has a chance to turn back and return to the shore.

But as he looks back, he sees for the first time all the things that made him unhappy. A bad relationship, a job he wanted to quit, negative people who were holding him back, old fears, habits and addictions.

We have all been there—that moment of decision when everything could change. You might have decided to stay where you were at times, or perhaps you engaged in negative self-talk. You might have kept a bad habit that was destroying you, and you had to either surrender or persevere and push ahead.

As Tony Robbins said:

"It is in our moments of decision that our destiny is shaped."

Imagine that you're hanging on to a branch in the middle of the rapids. You know you won't last much longer and you only have two choices. You can try to make it back to the shore you came from, or you can let go and try to make it to the other side. It comes down to three basic questions:

1. What are you really afraid of?
2. What is it about taking action that scares you so much that you are willing to suffer for it?
3. What price are you willing to pay to hold onto this fear?

In other words, if you are willing to tolerate your situation and everything that makes you unhappy, you can stay where you are. You may not live an empowered life, but on the other hand, you won't have to risk failure, embarrassment or losing to your ego.

Misery is cheap and anyone can afford it if they want it.

This brings us to the last question: How scared are you of staying where you are?

Are you stuck in a job that only pays minimum wage?

Are you overweight or out of shape?

Are you heavily in debt?

Do you spend time with people who are holding you back?

When you're stuck in the middle of the river, contemplating whether or not to push on, ask yourself what you have to lose.

What are you afraid of giving up? What fears are you facing?

Here is a list:

*   The fear of rejection

142 . SCOTT ALLAN

- The fear of failure
- The fear of humiliation
- The fear of loss
- The fear of the unknown
- The fear of not measuring up (or the fear of disappointment and inadequacy)
- The fear of criticism

You may have all these fears or just one of them. Regardless, we are going to break this down into a step-by-step process. By following this process, you can muster up the will to act.

Living your life beyond fear doesn't mean not having fear. We will always experience fear when our comfort zones are challenged or we are facing a crisis. What matters is how we react when fear is moving in strong.

Let Fear Go

"When a resolute young fellow steps up to the great bully, the world, and takes him boldly by the beard, he is often surprised to find it comes off in his hand, and that it was only tied on to scare away the timid adventurers."

— Ralph Waldo Emerson

Do you know what scares you? Is it public speaking? Talking to people you don't know? Discussing your feelings?

You can only confront your fears if you know what they are. You might be not be aware of this, but most of us go through our days trying to stay safe and avoid challenges. Unless we are forced to confront something, we procrastinate. But it is embracing fear that pushes us to grow.

All of us have massive potential, but we often fall short of it. Do you know why? We get to a point in life when we stop pursuing the challenge of breaking through our fears. Instead, we run for cover.

I encourage you to identify your fears. Be honest with yourself. "I am afraid of this." But do you know why?

This is the second step. It is one thing to identify what scares you, but you have to know why you're frightened by this. Let's use public speaking as an example. Most people shake when they get on stage. I know I do, and it used to be really bad. My voice would crack, and I had a pounding in my ears from all the blood rushing to my head. I nearly passed out once.

Then I asked myself, "Why am I afraid?" The answers were obvious. I had always feared being rejected and vulnerable. I had a lot of shame and I was afraid people could see right through me. That would mean they knew all my secrets.

I was afraid on stage because I had a lot of fear inside. My mind would scream:

"What if they can tell I'm a fake?"

"What if they boo me off?"

"What if I'm wrong or I make a mistake and forget what I'm talking about?"

What it came down to was the fear of being judged, criticized and discovered. When I could admit why I was afraid, I could turn it off. Exposing your fear means managing it.

Now, here are three strategies to help you break the fear keeping you scared.

1. Stop believing in your fears.

When we believe that our fears are greater than we are, it makes them larger than life. Our fears are not bigger than we are but, believing that they can defeat us, adds weight to the illusion of fear. Throughout this book I discussed several anecdotes to overcoming our fears and doubts and, to keep fear in perspective, we need to look at this way.

Fear is nothing more than False Evidence Appearing Real. Many of the future events we are convinced will happen rarely do. Sure, bad stuff does happen, and in many cases the things we never feared could happen too.

For example:

- You lose a job you were convinced was secure. What are you going to do?
- Your spouse walks out on you after twenty years of marriage. What are you going to do?
- The market crashes overnight and you lose 90% of your investments. What are you going to do?

The truth is, we waste too much time dreaming up fears of the future that may or may not happen. But who can predict what is going to happen today, tomorrow or in twenty years from now? There is no evidence to prove that 99% of our fears exist. The imagination is great at conjuring up illusions of what could happen.

The fear of failure? Yes, you will fail.

The fear of loss? Yes, you will lose something at least once in the next decade.

The fear of dying? Yes, that will happen too. Not today but, you can take great comfort in knowing most of your fears are false and some are destined to happen no matter what.

Our fears are only as great as our imaginations allow them to be. By knowing you can act and make choices in the present moment, it fills your mind and spirit with confidence.

2. Free Your Fears from Rejection.

We fear rejection on many fronts. Our internal rejection issues destroy opportunity, hold us back from achieving goals, and keep us living small when we should be living large.

Rejection is an issue that everyone deals with. In my coaching sessions, I have walked many people through the program to remove rejection fears from the equation. With this taken out, you are free to be yourself and take risks that once seemed impossible.

Imagine where you could be if you:

- Approach a company to apply for that job you really want.
- Ask someone for something you've always desired.
- Speak your mind without worrying what other people will think.
- Do it anyway when your fear is telling you to run.
- Talk back to your internal negative voices that are filling your head with lies about who you are.
- Start to count your wins and not your losses.
- Focus on building abundance and ignore your fear of scarcity.
- Put an end to your biggest negative behavior and adopt a set of positive values that trigger new habits.

Allow yourself to fail. More often we are so afraid to fail that we avoid trying. Our expectations and attitude from the beginning is "I have to be perfect before I try this." When we think this way, it reduces our motivation and drive to try. We defeat ourselves by refusing to accept our right to fail.

If you don't give yourself that room to grow, you'll never develop the skills you need to become confident.

Learning to fail is essential. You need to give yourself permission to learn. Confident people are not born, they are made through years of trial and error.

3.   Desensitize Your Fear

By knowing what scares you the most, you can challenge this fear again and again. You can condition your fears through a "rejection proof" strategy by getting out there and just doing it.

Jia Jiang, the founder of 100 Days of Rejection Therapy and the author of Rejection Proof, did exactly this. He went out and challenged himself to do 100 things that scared him. In many cases, it involved putting himself in certain situations that caused incredible discomfort.

Several of these daring challenges include:

Test drive an expensive car
Make an announcement on an airplane flight
Get a free room at a hotel
Challenge a CEO to a staring contest
Name my own price at Dollar Tree

By putting yourself in a situation in which the risk of rejection is high, we can desensitize ourselves to the fear. By getting rejected on purpose, you begin to lose the fear of this happening.

For example, you might be scared to approach strangers and strike up a conversation. However, I've found that most people enjoy a good chat with someone they don't even know. The next time you want to challenge your discomfort of approaching people, set a target for yourself. How many people can you meet in one hour, or one day? How will they react to you?

You might be surprised to know this, but many people feel the same way. We're afraid to ask, afraid to act, and afraid to be ourselves. Well, do it scared and make someone's day by starting a conversation.

Stepping out of the safety zone feels unnatural to us. Train your mind to set this aside and free yourself. Why be afraid when you could be making friends?

Facing up to the fears that have been keeping you scared for most of your life is not an easy challenge. But then again, living in fear and missing out on all the great things you could be experiencing is the sacrifice to giving into your fears. See fear as an opportunity to grow, because that is what it is and nothing more.

Ask yourself, "Where will I be if I take action?"

Who knows? You might end up with everything you ever dreamed of.

I know I did, but to get it, I had to say YES to my fears and NO to living life alone as recluse who was afraid to face the world.

So, be afraid.
Do it scared and take action today.
Say YES to the fear that holds you back.
Embrace fear as your companion on this journey.

As one of my favorite authors, the late Susan Jeffers, once said:

> "We must feel the fear and do it anyway."

Building Your Life
by Design

"Death is not the greatest loss in life. The greatest loss is what dies inside us while we live."

— Norman Cousins

We have covered a lot of material in this book. Just to recap, you learned how to:

- Integrate the 16 principles of world class achievers
- Design a personal mission statement
- Build a system of habits by sticking with a set routine
- Adopt a role-model to build a solid foundation
- Break through internal and external obstacles
- Determine your priorities and kill your distractions
- Turn failure into victory
- Release your resentment and turn negative thinking into a positive mindset
- Throw away excuses and develop the Steve Jobs approach, or new challenge approach.

Walt Disney once said, "All our dreams can come true, if we have the courage to pursue them."

I have always maintained the attitude that nothing in life is fixed or permanent. No matter where you are, how old you are, no matter where you live or what circumstances you have been thrown into, or what you've accomplished—or haven't—where you are today is the outcome of your life by design. Your decisions, thoughts, actions, and relationships have had a massive impact on the way your life has turned out so far.

If you are not where you want to be just yet, if you are still struggling to develop yourself to get to some place or accomplish a specific goal, you might want to consider the influences happening around you and within you.

Do you have compelling goals that build up your passion and make you want to stay up late and get up early?

Are you surrounding yourself with people who are supportive and can help you (and you can help them)?

Do you feel good about yourself emotionally, physically, and spiritually?

Do you have your priorities in place or are you still struggling with uncertainty?

Do you have a clear vision of the direction you want to take?

Are you committed to doing whatever it takes to break through your obstacles and succeed no matter what?

Design or Default: Your Life by Design

Everything you do is by design, whether it be default action or proactive. You—yes, you—can create anything you want. You can empower your life to attract every possible opportunity.

A life by design and not default means that we are taking intentional actions to change, shape and develop our future instead of allowing life to just happen. There is nothing more powerful than following through on a decision with consistent actions as opposed to just taking your chances.

Always remember: You're never a victim of your circumstances. You are the master of circumstances. While you may not be able to control what's happening, you can take charge of how to deal it.

In every situation there is a call to action. Will you do what is needed to respond when the time calls for it? Are you ready to take action on your goals?

No matter what takes place in the world around you, never allow circumstances to dictate your future.

Consider these situations:

What will you do if your business crashes and you have to start over?

What will you do if your spouse decides to divorce and you lose your job in the same week?

What will you do if you're in an accident and permanently injured?

The truth is, we don't know what challenges life will bring. One day things are fine, and the next you might be locked in a struggle to survive.

What we do know is that you can be the master of your actions. You can master your emotions and thus master the decisions that influence destiny. This is how you live by design and not default.

When we rely on default to work things out, it is like throwing chance to the wind and hoping for the best. In this case you have no control over the outcome and are relying on blind luck to get through.

Living by default works as long as everything works out, but in most cases, relying on good fortune or luck only goes so far. You usually end up serving someone else and stuck in a situation that makes you unhappy.

People who plan gain the most ground in their lives. They are able to make more money, have better jobs, travel more, and have the freedom and flexibility to do what they enjoy.

I'll make it simple for you: You're either living an empowered lifestyle governed by intentional action, or you exist to serve someone else's agenda. If it is the latter, and for many people it is, we can change this. There is always a new door to open and you have the key to unlock all the personal power you need.

By design, you are the master of your life.

By default, you become a slave to somebody else's plan.

This book is designed to get you thinking about your life and how you want it to be.

We can always maximize our quality of life by staying fixed on the things that matter most and avoiding whatever doesn't add value.

My hope in writing this book is that you may gain valuable tactics for boosting the quality of your life. You are meant to succeed, not just through achievements, but by helping others, spreading wisdom, and making others happy.

I'll leave you now with five valuable tips you can implement to squeeze every ounce of fulfillment out of your life. Not only will you improve your life, but you will also improve the lives of everyone around you.

To start living by design, here are the actionable steps you can take today.

Throw away your "life by default" attitude.

We fall into automated programming at an early stage. It starts with relying on someone else to make our decisions. We trust that those decisions made by others (parents, peers) are in our own best interest. But years later, we struggle to take control.

You might become helpless in certain situations and realize you have been living by default instead of by design (taking action and pushing toward your goals).

A massive shift in your attitude can change everything. This means thinking and acting in a way that is the opposite of how you have been doing things. Instead of trusting the universe to work things out, get up and put in the work yourself. The universe is busy with other things. Trusting the universe has your back and that you don't have to worry about a thing is setting yourself up for a fall.

Throw away the attitude that says it will all work out even if you do nothing. You can pray for the best, but then, as soon as you are done, get to work on building the best. Success is not an accident.

It is not a game of roulette where you might get lucky even if you do nothing. This book is based on a plan of action and you have to put what you know into play.

Keep pushing forward when the going gets tough.

Some days, my efforts seem to have little impact and I drain myself of energy when focused on negative thoughts. The journey is not always fun, and we struggle to get through some rough times. But the struggle is the victory.

It isn't reaching your destination that counts, but the walk you take to get there. Focus on the journey. When you get to the end of the road, the action is over. The thrill of the moment is right now and all the steps you take in this moment are adding up to your life's passion.

Stay focused on what matters most.

A question people often ask me is, "How can I know what matters most when everything feels important?"

My response is simple: "Focus on what feels right to you."

What is calling to you? Is it an idea, or a mission? In chapter one, I discussed at length defining your purpose in life. You will never discover what it really is if you are chasing everything.

You need to choose, and then pursue that idea or passion with relentless diligence. Stay focused on what makes a difference, not just in the moment because it feels right, but because you see the potential for building a successful future.

What matters most is having work that you love, enjoying the company of the people you work for, and the things you can do when your work sets you free. In other words, choose a profession that gives you the freedom to do what you want to do. You'll live a more empowered lifestyle. Not only will you be living your purpose, but you'll be embracing the best parts of this world.

Be aware of the obstacles keeping you stuck.

In chapter four, we discussed the roadblocks we have to deal with. By confronting these difficulties head on, we eliminate the attraction to procrastinate and avoid our difficulties.

Make a list of the challenges you have every day, even if it is something as simple as making a call or filling out a form. If something is blocking you, work to remove it and keep chipping away until it is done. This works for small obstacles as well as bigger ones. The bigger challenges may take longer but can be defeated, too.

Help people whenever possible.

When we are focused on building a life that counts, it is so easy to become self-absorbed. We might forget to watch out for the people who are struggling and could use our help.

Living your life by design is about helping others to reach their goals as well. A big part of your plan should be to build those vital relationships along the way. You will always be rewarded by helping others, even if that reward is not recognized in public.

Now, go do this thing. Empower your life in such a way that you set yourself up for success twenty years down the road. Begin today and start building that momentum. The opportunity you seek is grounded in the actions you take.

Until Next Time…

Together, I believe we can transcend any challenge and overcome all obstacles to create a better future.

Remember to give yourself the time to grow. You can begin by accepting the fact that there is no perfection in what we do. There is recovery and healing, learning and self-discovery, and subsequently, the branches of a new life are created.

We are on the precipice of a new world, and I take great comfort in knowing that I do not stand alone.

Be well, my friends, and may all the days shine brightly on you wherever you may travel.

Scott Allan

BEFORE YOU LEAVE...SUBSCRIBE TO MY FREE WEEKLY NEWSLETTER AND JOIN THE COMMUNITY OF 30,000+ LIFETIME LEARNERS!

Click here to subscribe or scan the QR code below.

"Don't ask what the world needs. Ask what makes you come alive and go do it. Because what the world needs is more people who have come alive."

— Howard Thurman

Books Change Lives.
Let's Change Yours Today.

Check out the complete
Bulletproof Mindset Mastery series *here by Scott Allan.*

Visit author.to/ScottAllanBooks or scan the QR Code below to
follow Scott Allan and stay up to date on future book releases

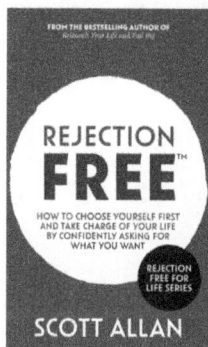

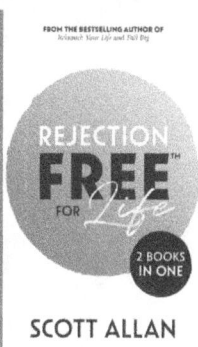

Begin Your Rejection Free Journey Today!

RejectionFreeBooks.com

Pathways to Mastery Series

Master Your Life One Book at a Time

Available where books and audiobooks are sold

Download this <u>Free Training</u> Manual—
Built For Stealth: Key Principles for
Building a Great Life

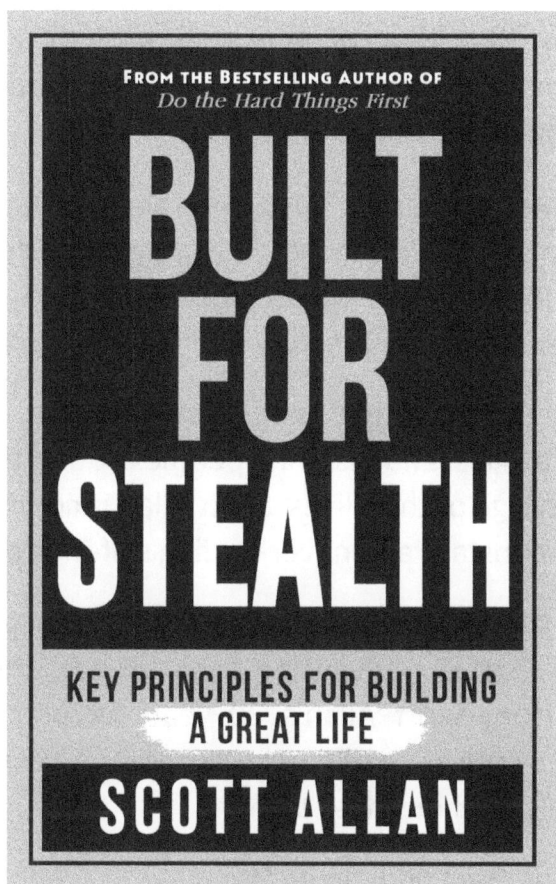

Available wherever <u>books</u>, <u>eBooks</u> and
audiobooks are sold.

About Scott Allan

Scott Allan is an international bestselling author of 25+ books in the area of personal growth and self-development. He is the author of **Fail Big**, **Undefeated,** and **Do the Hard Things First**.

As a former corporate business trainer in Japan, and Transformational Mindset Strategist, Scott has invested over 10,000 hours of practice and research into the areas of self-mastery and leadership training.

With an unrelenting passion for teaching, building critical life skills, and inspiring people around the world to take charge of their lives, Scott Allan is committed to a path of constant and never-ending self-improvement.

Many of the success strategies and self-empowerment material that is reinventing lives around the world evolves from Scott Allan's 20 years of practice and teaching critical skills to corporate executives, individuals, and business owners.

You can connect with Scott at:

scottallan@scottallanpublishing.com

Visit author.to/ScottAllanBooks to stay up to date on future book releases.

ScottAllan INTERNATIONAL SA